ST. THÉRÈSE
OF LISIEUX

MODERN SPIRITUAL MASTERS
Robert Ellsberg, Series Editor

This series introduces the writing and vision of some of the great spiritual masters of the twentieth century. Along with selections from their writings, each volume includes a comprehensive introduction, presenting the author's life and writings in context and drawing attention to points of special relevance to contemporary spirituality.

Some of these authors found a wide audience in their lifetimes. In other cases recognition has come long after their deaths. Some are rooted in long-established traditions of spirituality. Others charted new, untested paths. In each case, however, the authors in this series have engaged in a spiritual journey shaped by the influences and concerns of our age. Such concerns include the challenges of modern science, religious pluralism, secularism, and the quest for social justice.

At the dawn of a new millennium this series commends these modern spiritual masters, along with the saints and witnesses of previous centuries, as guides and companions to a new generation of seekers.

MODERN SPIRITUAL MASTERS SERIES

St. Thérèse of Lisieux

Essential Writings

Selected with
an Introduction by
MARY FROHLICH

ORBIS BOOKS

Maryknoll, New York 10545

Founded in 1970, Orbis Books endeavors to publish works that enlighten the mind, nourish the spirit, and challenge the conscience. The publishing arm of the Maryknoll Fathers & Brothers, Orbis seeks to explore the global dimensions of the Christian faith and mission, to invite dialogue with diverse cultures and religious traditions, and to serve the cause of reconciliation and peace. The books published reflect the views of their authors and do not represent the official position of the Maryknoll Society. To learn more about Maryknoll and Orbis Books, please visit our website at www.maryknoll.org.

Copyright © 2003 by the Institute of Carmelite Studies

Introduction copyright © 2003 by Mary Frohlich

Published by Orbis Books, Maryknoll, NY 10545-0308

Manufactured in the United States of America

Library of Congress Cataloging-in-Publication Data
Thérèse, de Lisieux, Saint, 1873–1897.
   [Selections. English. 2003]
   St. Thérèse of Lisieux : essential writings / selected with an
introduction by Mary Frohlich.
     p. cm. – (Modern spiritual masters series)
   ISBN 1-57075-469-1 (pbk.)
   1. Thérèse, de Lisieux, Saint, 1873-1897. 2. Spiritual
life – Catholic Church. I. Frohlich, Mary. II. Title. III. Series.
BX4700.T5 A25 2003
282'.092 – dc21
                              2002152356

Contents

Chronology of the Life of St. Thérèse of Lisieux

1873   *January 2*. Marie-Françoise-Thérèse Martin is born in Alençon, Normandy, France.

March 15 or 16. Sent to live with a peasant wet-nurse, Rose Taillé.

1874   *April 2*. Returns to family home.

1877   *August 29*. When their mother dies, Thérèse takes older sister Pauline as "second Mama."

November 16. The family settles in Lisieux at Les Buissonnets.

1881   *October 3*. Thérèse begins as a day student at the Benedictine Abbey.

1882   *October 2*. Pauline Martin, Thérèse's "second Mama," enters Carmel.

1883   *March 25 (Easter Sunday)*. Thérèse falls sick with trembling and hallucinations.

May 13 (Pentecost Sunday). Sees "the Virgin of the Smile" and is cured.

1884   *May 8*. First Communion.

1886   *December 25*. "Christmas Conversion"; discovers capacity for charity.

1887   *May 29 (Pentecost Sunday)*. Asks and receives her father's permission to enter Carmel.

September 1. Learns that "her sinner," Henri Pranzini, has kissed the cross before being executed.

1887   *November 4–December 2.* Pilgrimage to Rome, during which Thérèse asks the pope's permission to enter Carmel.

December 28. Definitive permission is given for her to enter Carmel.

1888   *April 9.* Thérèse enters Lisieux Carmel.

June 23. Her father's illness begins to manifest itself in bizarre behavior.

1889   *January 10.* Enters Novitiate; takes name, "Thérèse of the Child Jesus and of the Holy Face."

1890   *September 8.* Profession of Vows.

1893   *February 2.* First poem.

February 20. Mother Agnes (Thérèse's sister Pauline) is elected prioress; Thérèse is named assistant to the novice mistress.

1894   *January 21.* Writes and plays the title role in her first drama, "The Mission of Joan of Arc."

Spring. First manifestations of Thérèse's adult tubercular infection.

July 29. Death of Louis Martin.

1895   *January 21.* Writes and plays the title role in "Joan of Arc Accomplishes Her Mission"; her paper costume nearly catches on fire.

June 9 (Trinity Sunday). Composes her "Act of Oblation to Merciful Love."

October 17. Receives her first "spiritual brother," Abbé Bellière.

1896   *January 20.* Presents Manuscript A of *Story of a Soul* to Mother Agnes.

1896   *April 2–3 (night between Holy Thursday and Good Friday).* Coughs up a large quantity of blood, indicating tubercular illness is far advanced.

       April 5 (Easter Sunday). Enters the "Night of Faith."

       May 30. Receives her second "spiritual brother," Père Roulland.

       September 8. On yearly retreat, writes Manuscript B of *Story of a Soul.*

1897   *March.* The gravity of Thérèse's illness becomes apparent; she is forced to begin withdrawing from normal activity.

       April 6. Mother Agnes begins to record the "Last Conversations."

       April 21. Leo Taxil reveals his "Diana Vaughan" fraud in front of a picture of Thérèse playing Joan of Arc.

       June 3. Thérèse begins Manuscript C of *Story of a Soul.*

       July 8. As her suffering reaches extreme levels, Thérèse is moved to the infirmary.

       July 30. Receives sacrament of Extreme Unction.

       August 19. Last Holy Communion.

       August 25. Last letter — an inscription on a picture for Abbé Bellière.

       September 30. Thérèse dies.

1898   *September 30. Story of a Soul* published in French.

1923   *April 29.* Beatification.

1925   *May 17.* Canonization.

1997   *October 19 (Mission Sunday).* Named "Doctor of the Church."

Sources

LC   *St. Thérèse of Lisieux: Her Last Conversations.* Trans. John Clarke, O.C.D. Washington, D.C.: Institute of Carmelite Studies, 1977.

LT   *Letters of St. Thérèse of Lisieux.* Trans. John Clarke, O.C.D. Washington, D.C.: Institute of Carmelite Studies. Volume 1, 1982; Volume 2, 1988.

PN   *The Poetry of Saint Thérèse of Lisieux.* Trans. Donald Kinney, O.C.D. Washington, D.C.: Institute of Carmelite Studies, 1996.

RP   Translated by the editor from: *Édition Critique des Oeuvres Complètes de Sainte Thérèse de l'Enfant-Jésus et de la Sainte-Face.* Nouvelle édition du centenaire. Vol. 6: *Récréations Pieuses — Prières.* Paris: Desclée de Brouwer, Éditions de Cerf, 1992.

SS   *Story of a Soul: The Autobiography of St. Thérèse of Lisieux.* 3rd ed. Trans. John Clarke, O.C.D. Washington, D.C.: Institute of Carmelite Studies, 1996.

Introduction

The woman who is known to us as St. Thérèse of Lisieux spent all but about two weeks of her life in a small region of northwest France, and during her final nine years she never left the grounds of her Carmelite cloister — an enclosed space of no more than a few city blocks. Her one "trip abroad," taken with her father and sister when she was just fourteen years old, was a structured group pilgrimage to Rome. Yet very soon after her death, Thérèse and her story began to cross geographical and cultural boundaries with astonishing rapidity. By 1925, when she was officially declared a saint of the Roman Catholic Church, her autobiographical *Story of a Soul* had already been translated into twenty languages. By the year 1957 that number had reached fifty-four; today, it is undoubtedly even higher. In every corner of the globe, one will find some form of shrine to St. Thérèse in many Roman Catholic churches. A recent worldwide tour of her relics drew crowds in the tens of thousands at nearly every stop.

"The Little Flower": Simple or Complex?

Thérèse is probably best known by the title of "The Little Flower." This derives from a passage near the beginning of *Story of a Soul* where she compares herself to a humble little flower of the meadow. She affirms that she is not one of the gorgeous, outstanding flowers to which people flock to ooh and ah, but rather one among the throngs of ordinary little flowers who together praise God simply with their tiny arrays of ornament and perfume. Part of the vast appeal of this image is that it enables each reader or hearer to identify with Thérèse. When we are honest with ourselves, each of us knows that we, too, are "little flowers" whose lives and talents are more often than not ordinary and humdrum. The image of the little flower is an example of Thérèse's genius for sisterhood; she places herself as an equal in the midst of the masses of simple folk who will never be specially noticed or acclaimed. In doing so, she affirms and embraces the capability of each one to follow her in her "little way" of sanctity.

Yet today we know that Thérèse's life has, in fact, been lifted far above the crowds. She has been named not only a saint, but a Doctor of the Church; a huge basilica in her honor crowns the highest hill in Lisieux; she is special patroness of both France and the missions; thousands of churches and dozens of religious congregations are named for her around the world. The list could go on. There is a great paradox here: the climax of her utmost simplicity and humility turns out to be an enormous explosion of visibility and honor. Cynics might assert that this was exactly what she really wanted; her constant affirmations of "littleness," in this view, were a case of "protesting too much" that reveals an intense hunger for greatness.

In fact, Thérèse herself acknowledged as much. In one of the most celebrated passages of *Story of a Soul,* she wrote that she passionately desired to be warrior, priest, apostle, doctor of the Church, martyr, crusader, and papal guard as well as Carmelite, spouse, and mother of souls! Finding herself literally tortured by the intensity of these desires, she came to peace only when she was graced with the discovery of her true vocation: to be "love in the heart of the Church." This little vignette puts on display for us a fundamental truth about the human soul: when we come to rest in God, we are simple, singlehearted creatures; but the path to that simplicity, for each one of us, is complex, often tortuous, fraught with painfully conflicting desires and dreams. Thérèse was as human as any of us. She too, therefore, was a complex person who had to work through her personal versions of narcissism, illusion, sin, and inner and outer conflict.

In selecting and organizing texts for this anthology, one of my goals was to open up for readers some of the complexity of Thérèse's life and spirituality. This may seem odd, since I would affirm as clearly as anyone else that her ultimate gift to us is to show us how to fill our ordinary daily lives with the utmost simplicity of love for God. That part of her message, however, has already been proclaimed far and wide. Less well known are the contours of the human journey, the crucible in which that spirituality came to birth. Thérèse has sometimes been dismissed, especially by people of higher levels of education and sophistication, on the grounds that her protected and childlike life had little in common with their own. I hope that this anthology will help readers to know more about the often complex and demanding circumstances in which Thérèse articulated her "simple" spirituality.

Thérèse's Life and Context

Thérèse was born January 2, 1873, as the ninth and last child of Louis and Zélie Martin. As young people, both Louis and Zélie had applied unsuccessfully to religious communities. Subsequently each had lived for some years as a single person while establishing a business in the small French town of Alençon, Normandy. Louis had become a successful jeweler, Zélie an even more successful producer and distributor of the famous "point d'Alençon" lace. When they married (at a somewhat later age than the norm), Louis at first proposed that they live as "brother and sister" rather than engage in sexual relations. After some months, however, his spiritual director convinced him that their call was to a more normal marital life, including openness to children. The first child, Marie, arrived in 1860 and from then until 1873 there was a new baby in the Martin household every year or two. Louis and Zélie loved being parents and received each child with great joy. Tragically, their home was also invaded by profound sorrow; for during the six years prior to Thérèse's birth, three Martin infants and a five-year-old daughter succumbed to illnesses.

Thus, the infant Thérèse was welcomed into life with much love but also, most likely, with an undercurrent of deep anxiety on the part of her parents. Having so recently watched three of her babies waste away and die, Zélie Martin was deeply disturbed when she saw similar symptoms beginning to develop in Thérèse. Perhaps due to some physical condition of Thérèse or of Zélie (who, only a few years later, would die of breast cancer), or perhaps in a psychological reaction to Zélie's anxiety, two-month-old Thérèse became unable to take nourishment from her mother's breast. The starving and distraught baby was saved in the nick of time by the arrival of Rose Taillé, a robust peasant wet-nurse. Rose took Thérèse with her back to her sunny farm, where Thérèse thrived and grew. She did not return to live with her own family until she was fifteen months old.

When Thérèse rejoined the Martin household in April of 1874 she was greeted by four older sisters: Marie (b. 1860), Pauline (b. 1861), Léonie (b. 1863), and Céline (b. 1869). Marie and Pauline were already teenagers and so naturally took on a semi-motherly role toward their littlest sister. Céline, just three years older than Thérèse, soon became her bosom companion. Léonie, the middle child, never quite seemed to fit in and was already beginning her career as a lifelong source of worry for the family.

The Religious Milieu of the Time

The Martin family, like many bourgeois French Catholics of the time, lived a largely inward-facing life, creating a comfortable and pious world of its own within the confines of the family home. With family members having few opportunities for serious interaction with others, relationships within such families tended to be super-invested with emotional freight. At its best, this lifestyle could provide a safe environment for expression of a rich and delicate affectivity; at worst, it could be subtly manipulative or even grossly oppressive. Thérèse's early affective development was shaped by both the best and the worst potentials of this pattern.

All five Martin girls eventually became nuns — Léonie in the Visitation, the other four in Lisieux Carmel. This was the fruit of a family lifestyle in which an intense quest for holiness was woven into every aspect of daily life. The larger context of this, again, was the Catholic culture of the time. Devout French Catholics of the late nineteenth century were still reacting to the shock of the French revolution, in which the privileges and property of the Church had been violently wrested away by advocates of a radically secularistic and atheistic philosophy. Almost a hundred years later, many French Catholics remained entirely unreconciled to the new reality. They still clung fiercely to hope of a return of the "good old days" when monarchy and Church were two arms of a single power structure committed to maintaining France in its proud role of ecclesiastical and imperial leadership. Politically, this ideology was becoming increasingly out of touch with reality; by 1890, even the pope was advocating the *ralliement* — a policy of working with the secularized governments rather than attempting to dislodge them. At the grassroots level, however, many Catholics still configured their personal lives in terms of a black-and-white division between a holy, Church-centered life and the utter moral corruption they perceived in the mainstream culture. This had several consequences for spirituality. One was the tendency, described above, to turn inward and establish a separate, purified world of home, family, and Church with minimal outside contact. Another was the conviction that the duty of a good Catholic was to "repair" the damage done by the blasphemers by engaging in the maximum number of pious acts. Taking this one step further, the truly holy person was seen as one who prayed to take on the fullest form of reparation by becoming a "victim soul" whose personal suffering would make up for the horrors committed against God and the Church.

The Martin girls were raised within this mentality. Children of pious families were taught to take pride in counting up the number of their prayers, devotions, good deeds, acts of humility, little acceptances of suffering, and so on. Not surprisingly, this could lead to intense competition and pressure to conform, as well as a lot of judgmental gossip. Those who were most caught up in this spirituality often suffered from the affliction of scruples — an all-consuming anxiety that one might be doing something wrong, or in the wrong way, or not doing enough, and that this has radically alienated one from God. Customs and attitudes like these must be recognized as forming the backdrop of Thérèse's spiritual development. This cultural spirituality, with its particular strengths as well as its very evident distortions, was the raw material that Thérèse had to transform in the crucible of her personal quest for authentic holiness.

Childhood Trauma and Grace

When Thérèse was only four years old, Zélie Martin succumbed to breast cancer. Shortly thereafter, Louis Martin sold his jewelry business and moved the family to Lisieux, where they could be close to Zélie's brother Isidore Guérin and his family. The family settled in a large, comfortable home on the outskirts of town; the little estate had the title "Les Buissonnets" (loosely translated, "The Bushes"; by connotation, a place of taking one's ease.) It was in these pleasant surroundings that Thérèse spent the rest of her childhood prior to entering the monastery.

On the day of her mother's burial, Thérèse had announced that older sister Pauline would be her "new mama." It is important to realize that psychologically speaking, Zélie's death was actually Thérèse's third traumatic experience of mother-loss. Scars were necessarily left by the inability to form the nursing bond with her birth-mother at age two months, followed by bonding and then removal from her wet-nurse at age fifteen months. It is not surprising, then, that Pauline's entrance to Carmel in October of 1882, when Thérèse was nine years old, left the little girl deeply distraught. In those days entrance to Carmel meant that the nun would never again leave the cloister, and family visits were always highly formal group affairs with a barrier separating the religious from her lay family. Once again, Thérèse had lost her primary mothering relationship.

The period immediately following this involves one of the most debated incidents in Thérèse's short life. On Easter Sunday (March 25, 1883), Thérèse fell ill with trembling, convulsions, and hallucinations. These and other disturbing symptoms continued for seven weeks, with only a brief remission in April, during which she was able to attend the ceremony for Pauline's reception of the habit at Carmel. The doctors were mystified by the bizarre illness. Then on Pentecost Sunday (May 13, 1883), while Marie and Léonie prayed beside her sickbed, Thérèse looked at a statue of the Virgin Mary and saw Mother Mary smiling upon her beatifically. She was instantly cured; while some weakness remained for a short time, she was soon able to return to normal activities.

Was this a psychosomatic illness—a neurotic reaction to the repeated trauma of mother-loss? Or is this the story of an undiagnosed physical illness followed by a miraculous cure? While there can be no complete certainty, recent research suggests the following as a likely scenario.* Thérèse had started school as a day student at the Benedictine Abbey one year before Pauline entered Carmel. This was her first experience of prolonged time outside the home and in the presence of a large number of children of varied backgrounds. Epidemiologists note that in regions where the tuberculosis bacterium is endemic, the most common time for children to contract the disease is during their first year of school. The described symptoms of Thérèse's

---

*This theory is developed by Robert Masson in *Souffrance des hommes: Un psychiatre interroge Thérèse de Lisieux* (Versailles: Saint-Paul, 1997).

strange childhood illness, in fact, are congruent with those of an
encephalitis resulting from infection of the brain by tuberculosis. It is possible for such an infection to go into remission and
then to reappear many years later.

It is well known that Thérèse died of tuberculosis at the age
of twenty-four; what is not known is when she contracted it.
This scenario would suggest a childhood infection, perhaps fa-
cilitated by her emotional fragility in the face of starting school
(which was far from a pleasant experience for her) and losing
her "mama" Pauline. It would also allow for both physiological
and spiritual explanations for her "cure." On the physiological level, such remissions are always possible while often not
able to be fully accounted for. On the spiritual level, there is no
doubt that the experience of the "Virgin of the Smile" was a
turning point in Thérèse's life. This grace of the Virgin Mother's
smile provided her with a lifelong resource for transforming
her deep wound of mother-loss into an open space of compassionate love for others. Thus, there is no contradiction between
affirming that this was probably a physiological illness and remission, and also affirming that it was deeply woven into the
story of God's grace at work in her life.

Thérèse's "Christmas Conversion"

The next major turning point took place about three years later,
when Thérèse was on the verge of turning fourteen. When the
family returned home after Midnight Mass of Christmas, 1886,
Thérèse immediately ran to the fireplace expecting to delight in
the customary little gifts placed in the shoes that children left
out for this purpose. Louis Martin, tired and out of sorts from
the lateness of the hour, made a harsh comment about how
inappropriate it was for such a big girl to continue this childish custom. Normally, Thérèse would have reacted with angry
tears, and the ensuing unpleasant scene would have ruined the
special night for everyone. Instead, however, she discovered
within herself the grace to respond with charity. She simply

smiled, went on showing delight in the gifts, and made an extra effort to cheer up her father. Later on she would write that this very small and ordinary family incident was one of the greatest events of grace in her life. It was, for her, a moment of profound conversion: she had begun to discover the art of transforming narcissistic hurt into outpoured love.

Very quickly, Thérèse realized the vocation to apply this discovery of charity on a scale far beyond her immediate family. When shortly after this the notorious murderer Henri Pranzini flaunted his lack of repentance for his deeds, Thérèse took it upon herself to pray and make sacrifices for him. When he kissed the cross just moments before his execution, Thérèse was confirmed in her certainty that she had a calling to pray and sacrifice for sinners.

The Determination of a Fourteen-Year-Old

During the fall before Thérèse's "Christmas conversion," older sister Marie had joined Pauline at the Lisieux Carmel. Now, Thérèse became inspired with the conviction that she too was called to enter Carmel. On Pentecost Sunday (May 29, 1887), fourteen-year-old Thérèse asked her father for permission to pursue this course of action. Her dream was to be in Carmel by the following Christmas — the anniversary of her special experience of grace. With sorrow at the imminent loss of his "Little Queen" (Louis's pet name for Thérèse), yet also with a touch of pride in her maturity and fervor, he gave his consent. Receiving permission from other authorities, however, was much more challenging. It was almost unheard of for one so young to be allowed to enter, and in addition it was contrary to the norm to have three blood sisters in one Carmel. Permission was refused, first by the priest in charge of the monastery and then by the local bishop. Thérèse was devastated, but she did not give up. At that very time Louis Martin was planning to join a group making a November pilgrimage to Rome; Thérèse and her sister Céline were also invited to participate. Thérèse conceived the plan of taking her quest for permission to enter Carmel to the pope himself.

The pilgrimage to Rome, which also included stops at several other famous French and Italian cities, took place between November 4 and December 2, 1887. The trip was a great adventure for the teenage Thérèse, who had never traveled anywhere except for vacations at the Normandy seashore. Many of the other pilgrims were priests, whose frequently less-than-edifying behavior shocked her and fueled a lifelong conviction about the necessity of praying for priests. For her the highlight of the trip, however, was the scheduled audience with Pope Leo XIII on November 20. Despite explicit instructions not to attempt to speak to the pope during the reception of individual blessings, Thérèse hurriedly poured out her request for permission to enter Carmel. His reply — "You will enter if God wills it!" — was not the total endorsement she had hoped for. Bitterly disappointed, Thérèse began the journey home convinced that God had abandoned her. It was only some weeks later that she learned that the pope's words had been prophetic, for on December 28 the bishop's permission for her to enter Carmel arrived.

Thérèse of the Child Jesus and of the Holy Face

On April 9, 1888, Thérèse Martin became a postulant in Lisieux Carmel. She originally took the title "Thérèse of the Child Jesus"; less than a year later, when she received the habit, she expanded that to "Thérèse of the Child Jesus and of the Holy Face." Each part of this title expresses basic aspects of her spirituality that were already well established by the time of her entrance to the monastery.

No sooner had Thérèse entered Carmel than she was faced with a disturbing family crisis. Louis Martin (sixty-four years old at the time) began to manifest signs of dementia, recounting and even acting out strange, hallucinatory events. As the months went by this became so serious that he had to be placed in a mental hospital, for fear that he would harm someone during his delusional episodes. The whole family was deeply humiliated by his illness, especially since at that time the cultural attitude was that mental illness was most likely the fruit of either moral turpitude or inferior heredity. Thérèse, who had always admired her father greatly and, especially after the death of her mother, relied on him emotionally, suffered deeply. His affliction forced her into profound pondering on the mystery of the suffering of the just. Searching scriptures and tradition, Thérèse (still only a novice and a teenager) found much solace and wisdom in the "suffering servant" texts of Isaiah and in the writings of John of the Cross.

It was in her devotion to the Holy Face, however, that her fullest spiritual response to her father's suffering crystallized. The responsive, loving face of someone who cares for us is what the child in each of us desires most deeply. Thérèse longed to bask in her father's loving gaze, and even more profoundly in that of her God. Yet her father's cherished face, like the beloved face of Jesus, was now seen to be contorted by horrible suffering. In each case, their true personhood was hidden, humiliated, seemingly even totally lost. In this crucible, Thérèse learned that our calling, in devotion to the Holy Face, is to remain faithful in love even when the desired face seems to be turned completely away, abandoning us. In faith, we must affirm the belief that the just one is actually offering himself in purest love. His suffering and alienation is the prelude to a greater communion, into which we too will be invited if we keep our own faces faithfully turned toward the Beloved. These lessons that Thérèse learned so early in her life in Carmel through her father's passion would serve her well in her own hour of agony to come.

The Maturation of a Spirituality

Louis Martin did not die until July of 1894. By that time, Thérèse was already showing early signs of the tubercular illness that would take her life only three and a half years later. Those final years were a period of extraordinary spiritual insight and creativity for Thérèse. As she celebrated her twenty-first birthday on January 2, 1894, she was truly entering upon her spiritual and literary majority. All of her eight plays, all but one of her fifty-four poems, and all three manuscripts that formed her famous *Story of a Soul* were composed between January of 1894 and July of 1897.

In many ways, the richest and most succinct testament of Thérèse's spiritual sojourn is her "Act of Oblation to Merciful Love," which she composed on Trinity Sunday in June of 1895. Therein she wrote: "In order to live in one single act of perfect Love, I OFFER MYSELF AS A VICTIM OF HOLOCAUST TO YOUR MERCIFUL LOVE, asking You to consume me incessantly, allowing the waves of *infinite tenderness* shut up within You to overflow into my soul, and that thus I may become a *martyr* of Your *Love,* O my God!" In this Oblation, Thérèse both appropriated and transformed the spirituality of reparation which was common within her cultural milieu. Whereas others typically offered themselves as "victims of divine justice" and prayed to suffer, Thérèse offered herself as a sacrifice to be consumed by love. She gave thanks for her suffering because it was a share in the passion of Christ, but what she asked God for was "to work for *Your Love* alone, with the one purpose of pleasing you, consoling Your Sacred Heart, and saving souls who will love You eternally." Thérèse understood clearly the core Christian meaning of martyrdom as not being focused on suffering, but rather on totally committed love that stops at nothing to manifest and fulfill that love.

The Night of Nothingness

All these profound spiritual insights and aspirations, born of all the days of grace and pain which she had lived up to that point, were to be radically put to the test by the events of the final eighteen months of Thérèse's life. On the night between Holy Thursday and Good Friday of 1896, Thérèse coughed up a large quantity of blood. People of that era, in which tuberculosis was rampant, knew from experience that this was a sign that the disease was far advanced and that an agonizing death was likely to be not far off. Perhaps it was exactly because they knew this so well that they tried to deny it as long as possible. Thérèse wanted to continue carrying out all her normal obligations, and her prioress concurred. Meanwhile, she received very little treatment for her disease, and none that was at all effective.

At the same time, her intensifying physical suffering was compounded by an even more profound spiritual trial; for on Easter Sunday she was suddenly overtaken by a complete loss of any consoling sense of God's presence. She spent the last eighteen months of her life in this "thick darkness," a "night of nothingness," which was also at times accompanied by the strongest temptations to blaspheme God and abandon faith. She who had always lived with such careful and minute attention to piety — and who, at age fifteen, had been told by a confessor that she had never committed a mortal sin — now found herself eating at the same table as "poor sinners." It was here, reduced to nothingness in her own eyes, that she learned the most demanding lessons of divine compassion.

A bizarre incident that occurred during this final period gives us a telling view of the political and spiritual milieu in which Thérèse was living, as well as of the piling up of many levels of stress that marked her last months. Between 1893 and 1897 the French Catholic press had been following with much fascination the story of Diana Vaughan, a young American woman who had been raised from childhood to be a "high priestess" of a Luciferian sect of freemasons. During this same period, the political tension between the anticlerical forces and the monarchist Catholics was reaching new highs; and many Catholics (including Thérèse's uncle Isidore Guérin, publisher of a right-wing journal), made little distinction between anticlericalism, Satanism, and freemasonry. In May of 1895 the journal *La Croix* published a letter exhorting Catholics to pray to Joan of Arc for Diana's conversion; in June her conversion was triumphantly reported; and in July the imminent publication of her memoirs was announced. Bulletins reporting Miss Vaughan's activities debunking her former freemason colleagues began to appear with regularity.

Meanwhile, in January of 1895, Thérèse had written and played the title role in her second play about the life of Joan of Arc. The cult of Joan, savior of France, had been propagated with much fervor ever since the humiliating defeat of France in the Franco-Prussian war of 1871. Recognizing Thérèse's literary talents, and excited by the real-life drama of Diana Vaughan, the prioress asked Thérèse to write a play about it. Thérèse wrote "The Triumph of Humility," which depicts Diana's story as a lurid struggle with demons who ultimately are vanquished by Christ's cross and our humility. The play expresses the hope that Diana might eventually become a Carmelite nun in "our little Carmel." Shortly after this play was performed in June of 1896, the prioress asked Thérèse to inscribe a photograph of Thérèse playing Joan of Arc so that it could be sent to Diana Vaughan to congratulate her on her conversion. Within a few weeks, the Carmel received a cordial note of thanks from Miss Vaughan.

Despite the general enthusiasm for the story, there was increasing concern about that fact that no one had ever actually seen Diana Vaughan. Finally, to allay these concerns, her spokesman — Leo Taxil, another former freemason — arranged a presentation on April 19, 1987. He would speak first, and then Miss Vaughan would make her appearance. As a backdrop, he projected a huge picture of a Carmelite nun — in fact, Thérèse — acting the part of Joan of Arc. In front of a large crowd, Taxil dramatically revealed that the Diana Vaughan story was a fraud. He had made it all up as part of an anticlericalist campaign to demonstrate the foolish gullibility of the pious.

Not surprisingly, a great outpouring of anger and revilement against Taxil and his ilk ensued. But for Thérèse, the shock was more personal. She had hidden herself away in Carmel to give witness to the glories of Christ, and now instead her face was associated with a sacrilegious deception that was the talk of the whole world. Her personal imaginary drama of female spiritual heroism, interwoven with the stories of both Joan of Arc and Diana Vaughan, had been publicly impugned in the most devastating way. We must remember that this was occurring at a moment in her life when she was already in deep spiritual darkness — bordering on loss of faith — and experiencing unrelenting pain from the effects of her physical illness. Suddenly her inner "dark night" included a totally unexpected public and political humiliation as well.

Thérèse's Mission

Interestingly, it is during these same final months that Thérèse's commitment and insight into her own mission deepened profoundly. She had long desired to be a missionary in the literal sense and had volunteered to be sent to the Carmel in Hanoi. Her health proved too weak for this transfer, but meanwhile she was given two young missionary priests as "spiritual brothers" to pray for. It is in her final letters to Père Roulland and Abbé Bellière that we see the full development of her conviction that her work of love and prayer will continue through eternity. It is as if, in her deepening night, the boundary between time and eternity was dissolved; she no longer fantasized about what she might accomplish by future heroic action, but instead simply believed from the core of her being that the life of love that is the grace of the present moment is embraced, fulfilled, and made forever fruitful in the eternity of God.

The last three months of Thérèse's life were spent in horrifying and constantly increasing physical pain. Following monastic custom, she was given no painkillers at all until she was in the full death agony; then she received a single spoonful of morphine syrup. The mercy of death finally came for her on the evening of September 30, 1897.

Yet in a true sense, life for Thérèse had just begun. Only a little more than a year later, her *Story of a Soul* (along with some of her letters and poetry) was published. Within ten years thirty-three thousand copies of the French edition had been distributed, and editions in six other European languages were also circulating. As the movement for her canonization caught fire, these numbers swelled rapidly. In one of the fastest canonization procedures in modern times, she was named "Venerable" in 1921, "Blessed" in 1923, and "Saint" in 1925. To date, hundreds of thousands of copies of her writings have been produced in sixty or more languages. This wide distribution, plus the development of a thriving popular devotion that is centered in belief in the as-tonishing efficacy of her prayers, has made Thérèse very much a "living saint" in the hearts and minds of millions of people worldwide. Her life goes on, in and around us.

Thérèse's Intercultural Appeal

What is it about this woman that has enabled her to exer-cise such remarkable international and intercultural appeal? Ultimately, of course, the answer has to be that it is her sanc-tity itself. One who is close to God is close to all humanity. Yet many saints, great and small, have comparatively little noticeable impact beyond their immediate localities. Thérèse's boundary-crossing appeal may have to do with three attributes that she embodied with a unique quality of transparency: childlikeness; the transformation of suffering into love; and sisterhood.

Childlikeness

Many who know little else about Thérèse have heard of her under her first religious title, "Thérèse of the Child Jesus." Hu-mans (and, indeed, all animals whose offspring require care) have an inbuilt tendency to respond with affection and care to the young and needy. Spiritual traditions have built upon this by developing devotion to the infant Jesus and, even more profoundly, by promoting an attitude of childlikeness before God. Thérèse embraced both of these at the deepest level. For her, childlikeness meant an attitude of sheer trust — like that of a child who may have been naughty but who nevertheless runs straight to her parent without any doubt that she will be received lovingly. Since the experiences of being a child, of feeling affection for children, and of having childlike longings are universal, this aspect of Thérèse's spirituality travels easily across cultural boundaries.

Still, not everyone finds this idea of adopting a childlike persona before God and others endearing. There is, indeed, a risk that one who too enthusiastically claims childlikeness may be refusing to come to terms with the complexities and responsibilities of adulthood. Thérèse's appeal would be shallow if childlikeness were not balanced by other dimensions.

The Transformation of Suffering into Love

Until recently, few people knew much about Thérèse as a woman of suffering. While the basic fact of her painful death from tuberculosis at age twenty-four was well known, even this was often recounted in a very pious fashion that emphasized her sanctity while downplaying the enormity of her physical agony. In fact, as we have learned as we reviewed her life story, from infancy onward Thérèse suffered repeated traumas through both emotional loss and physical illness. Every episode of her spiritual sojourn was, at root, a costly struggle to allow grace to transform those sufferings into occasions of love. This is another universal element to which every human being can connect: everyone suffers, and everyone struggles to find meaning, hope, and love in their suffering.

Yet once again, some critique Thérèse on the grounds that her spirituality is grounded in a kind of narcissistic dramatization of the most minute wounds and triumphs of the self.

A classic example is the story she told of being splashed with water in the laundry and making of it an identification with Jesus' passion. Still, it is in just such small matters that most human beings must make their spiritual way day in and day out. Those who suffer, whether through the minutia of everyday affronts or in genuinely overwhelming agonies, can recognize in Thérèse a companion who knows intimately the path they are walking.

Sisterhood

In a way, to speak of Thérèse as "sister" summarizes all that has been said about her first two boundary-crossing qualities. Those who are drawn to Thérèse find in her a companion, a friend, a quiet presence, a support, who stands behind or beside one according to the need of the moment. She is strong with the fierceness of maternal or sisterly love, yet simple and unassuming as a fellow child of God. Finally, it is her quality of sisterhood that enables her to be received with joy in every culture.

•

Since Thérèse's *Story of a Soul* is so accessible, and indeed has probably already been read by most of those who take an interest in her, selections for this anthology draw heavily on her other writings — her letters, poems, and plays. Each of the seven chapters of the anthology is focused around one of Thérèse's core self-images or roles. Chapter 1 lifts out key stories about her childhood from *Story of a Soul,* thus offering us both an opportunity to get to know her formative story and an insight into the central place of "spiritual childhood" in her spirituality. Chapter 2 reveals the young Carmelite Thérèse as affectionate sister and friend, writing image-filled letters of support and counsel to her sister Céline, who was consigned to remaining home with their ill father. The third chapter gives us a deeper glimpse into the structure of Thérèse's imaginative world as it traces her childhood identification with Joan of Arc and its further development in the two plays that, as an adult, she penned about Joan's life. Chapter 4 explores the developing contours of her self-image as "Martyr of Divine Mercy," while chapter 5 is focused on Thérèse's core discovery of her vocation to be "love in the heart of the Church." Finally, the sixth and seventh chapters show Thérèse in the fullness of her ministry and mission as teacher, formator, spiritual sister, and emerging saint.

1

Thérèse,
Child of Sorrow and Grace

All the texts in this chapter come from "Manuscript A" of Story of a Soul. This manuscript was composed at the request of the prioress, Mother Agnes, between January of 1895 and January of 1896. Mother Agnes was, in fact, Thérèse's blood sister Pauline, whom she had taken as her "mama" at the time of their mother's death. Hearing Thérèse speak of the graces of her childhood, Agnes was inspired to ask her to write down these stories. It is primarily through these ingenuous narratives of a child's discovery of grace that so many thousands of people from around the world have been attracted to Thérèse's "little way."

"THE LITTLE FLOWER"

As Thérèse offers her famous metaphor of the "little flower," we see how she creatively weaves scripture, memory, and poetic image to explain her spiritual insight. At the end of this passage she applies the metaphor to her own family, referring to Louis and Zélie Martin as "stems" from whom nine "Lilies" have sprouted (four siblings already in heaven; three now with "the little flower" in Lisieux Carmel; the ninth, Léonie, in the Visitation Monastery).

It is to you, dear Mother, to you who are doubly my Mother, that I come to confide the story of my soul. The day you asked me to do this, it seemed to me it would distract my heart by too much concentration on myself, but since then Jesus has made me feel that in obeying simply, I would be pleasing Him; besides, I'm going to be doing only one thing: I shall begin to sing what I must sing eternally: *"The Mercies of the Lord."*

Before taking up my pen, I knelt before the statue of Mary (the one which has given so many proofs of the maternal preferences of heaven's Queen for our family), and I begged her to guide my hand that it trace no line displeasing to her. Then opening the Holy Gospels my eyes fell upon these words: "And going up a mountain, he called to him men of his *own choosing,* and they came to him" (Mark 3:13). This is the mystery of my vocation, my whole life, and especially the mystery of the privileges Jesus showered upon my soul. He does not call those who are worthy but those whom He *pleases* or as St. Paul says: "God will have mercy on whom he will have mercy, and he will show pity to whom he will show pity. So then there is question not of him who wills nor of him who runs, but of God showing mercy" (Romans 9:15–16).

I wondered for a long time why God has preferences, why all souls don't receive an equal amount of graces. I was surprised when I saw Him shower His extraordinary favors on saints who had offended Him, for instance, St. Paul and St. Augustine, and whom He forced, so to speak, to accept His graces. When reading the lives of the saints, I was puzzled at seeing how Our Lord was pleased to caress certain ones from the cradle to the grave, allowing no obstacle in their way when coming to Him, helping them with such favors that they were unable to soil the immaculate beauty of their baptismal robe. I wondered why poor savages died in great numbers without even having heard the name of God pronounced.

Jesus deigned to teach me this mystery. He set before me the book of nature; I understood how all the flowers He has created are beautiful, how the splendor of the rose and the whiteness of the Lily do not take away the perfume of the little violet or the delightful simplicity of the daisy. I understood that if all flowers wanted to be roses, nature would lose her springtime beauty, and the fields would no longer be decked out with little wild flowers.

And so it is in the world of souls, Jesus' garden. He willed to create great souls comparable to Lilies and roses, but He has created smaller ones and these must be content to be daisies or violets destined to give joy to God's glances when He looks down at his feet. Perfection consists in doing His will, in being what He wills us to be.

I understood, too, that Our Lord's love is revealed as perfectly in the most simple soul that resists His grace in nothing as in the most excellent soul; in fact, since the nature of love is to humble oneself, if all souls resembled those of the holy Doctors who illumined the Church with the clarity of their teachings, it seems God would not descend so low when coming to their heart. But He created the child who knows only how to make his feeble cries heard; He has created the poor savage who has nothing but the natural law to guide him. It is to their hearts that God deigns to lower Himself. These are the wild flowers whose simplicity attracts Him. When coming down in this way, God manifests His infinite grandeur. Just as the sun shines simultaneously on the tall cedars and on each little flower as though it were alone on the earth, so Our Lord is occupied particularly with each soul as though there were no others like it. And just as in nature all the seasons are arranged in such a way as to make the humblest daisy bloom on a set day, in the same way, everything works out for the good of each soul.

Perhaps you are wondering, dear Mother, with some astonishment where I am going from here, for up until now I've said nothing that resembles the story of my life. But you asked me to write under no constraint whatever would come into my mind. It is not, then, my life properly so called that I am going to write; it is my thoughts on the graces God deigned to grant me.

I find myself at a period in my life when I can cast a glance upon the past; my soul has matured in the crucible of exterior and interior trials. And now, like a flower strengthened by the storm, I can raise my head and see the words of Psalm 22 realized in me: "The Lord is my Shepherd, I shall not want; he makes me lie down in green pastures. He leads me beside still waters; he restores my soul. Even though I walk through the valley of the shadow of death, I fear no evil; for thou art with me.... " To me the Lord has always been "merciful and good, slow to anger and abounding in steadfast love" (Psalm 102:8).

It is with great happiness, then, that I come to sing the mercies of the Lord with you, dear Mother. It is for you alone I am writing the story of the *little flower* gathered by Jesus. I will talk freely and without any worries as to the numerous digressions I will make. A mother's heart understands her child even when it can but stammer, and so I'm sure of being understood by you, who formed my heart, offering it up to Jesus!

It seems to me that if a little flower could speak, it would tell simply what God has done for it without trying to hide its blessings. It would not say, under the pretext of a false humility, it is not beautiful or without perfume, that the sun has taken away its splendor and the storm has broken its stem when it knows that all this is untrue. The flower about to tell her story rejoices at having to publish the totally gratuitous gifts of Jesus. She knows that nothing in herself was capable of attracting the divine glances, and His mercy alone brought about everything that is good in her.

It was He who had her born in a holy soil, impregnated with a *virginal perfume*. It was He, too, who has her preceded by eight Lilies of dazzling whiteness. In His love He wished to preserve His little flower from the world's empoisoned breath. Hardly had her petals begun to unfold when this divine Savior transplanted her to Mount Carmel where already two Lilies, who had taken care of her in the springtime of her life, spread their sweet perfume. Seven years have passed by since the little flower took root in the garden of the Spouse of Virgins, and now *three* Lilies bloom in her presence. A little farther off another Lily expands under the eyes of Jesus. The two stems who brought these flowers into existence are now reunited for all eternity in the heavenly Fatherland. There they have found once again the four Lilies the earth had not seen develop. Oh! may Jesus deign not to allow a long time to pass on these strange shores for the flowers left in exile. May the Lily-plant be soon complete in Heaven! —SS 13–16

THE LITTLE IMP

Thérèse wrote that her life was divided into three distinct periods. The first encompassed the four and half years before her mother's death; the second, the approximately ten years before her "Christmas conversion" and decision to enter Carmel; the third, her Carmelite years. As she describes the happy milieu of her early childhood and the spirited character that began to manifest itself there, she quotes a letter her mother wrote when Thérèse was just three years old.

In the story of my soul, up until my entrance into Carmel, I distinguish three separate periods. The first is not the least fruitful in memories in spite of its short duration. It extends from the dawn of my reason till our dear Mother's departure for heaven....

God was pleased all through my life to surround me with *love,* and the first memories I have are stamped with smiles and the most tender caresses. But although He placed so much *love* near me, He also sent much love into my little heart, making it warm and affectionate. I loved Mama and Papa very much and showed my tenderness for them in a thousand ways, for I was very expressive....

Here is a passage from one of Mama's letters showing how good Céline was and how I was just the opposite. "My little

Céline is drawn to the practice of virtue; it's part of her nature; she is candid and has a horror of evil. As for the little imp, one doesn't know how things will go, she is so small, so thoughtless! Her intelligence is superior to Céline's, but she's less gentle and has a stubborn streak in her that is almost invincible; when she says '*no*' nothing can make her give in, and one could put her in the cellar a whole day and she'd sleep there rather than say 'yes.'

"But still she has a heart of gold; she is very lovable and frank; it's curious to see her running after me making her confession: 'Mama, I pushed Céline once, I hit her once, but I won't do it again.' (It's like this for everything she does.) Thursday evening we took a walk in the direction of the train station, and she wanted absolutely to go into the waiting room to go and see Pauline; she was running on ahead with a joy that was pleasant to see, but when she saw we had to return without getting on the train to go to visit Pauline, she cried all the way home."

—SS 16–17, 22

"I CHOOSE ALL!"

A small childhood incident, when big sister Léonie offers her little sisters Céline and Thérèse a gift, becomes a foreshadowing of Thérèse's future destiny.

One day, Léonie, thinking she was too big to be playing any longer with dolls, came to us with a basket filled with dresses and pretty pieces for making others; her doll was resting on top. "Here, my little sisters, choose; I'm giving you all this." Céline stretched out her hand and took a little ball of wool which pleased her. After a moment's reflection, I stretched out mine saying: "I choose all!" and I took the basket without further ceremony. Those who witnessed the scene saw nothing wrong and even Céline herself didn't dream of complaining....

This little incident of my childhood is a summary of my whole life; later on when perfection was set before me, I understood that to become a saint one had to suffer much, seek out always the most perfect thing to do, and forget self. I understood, too, there were many degrees of perfection and each soul was free to respond to the advances of Our Lord, to do little or much for Him, in a word, to choose among the sacrifices He was asking. Then, as in the days of my childhood, I cried out: "My God 'I choose all!' I don't want to be a saint by halves, I'm not afraid to suffer for You, I fear only one thing: to keep my own will; so take it, for 'I choose all' that You will!" — SS 27

THE SUNNY YEARS

Here we see how, during this first period of her life, Thérèse's impressionable soul was deeply formed by love of nature and by early training in charity and self-control.

Ah! how quickly those sunny years passed by, those years of my childhood, but what a sweet imprint they have left on my soul! I recall the days Papa used to bring us to the pavilion; the smallest details are impressed in my heart. I recall especially the Sunday walks when Mama used to accompany us. I still feel the profound and poetic impressions which were born in my soul at the sight of fields enameled with corn-flowers and all types of wild flowers. Already I was in love with the wide-open spaces. Space and the gigantic fir trees, the branches sweeping down to the ground, left in my heart an impression similar to the one I experience still today at the sight of nature.

We frequently met poor people on these long walks, and it was always little Thérèse who was put in charge of bringing them alms, which made her quite happy. Very often Papa, finding the walk too long for his little Queen, brought her back to the house before the others (which pleased her very much). And to console her, Céline filled her pretty little basket with daisies and gave them to her when she got back; but alas! grandmother found her granddaughter had too many, so she took a large part of them for her statue of the Blessed Virgin. This didn't please little Thérèse, but she kept from saying anything, having got into the habit of not complaining ever, even when they took what belonged to her or when she was accused unjustly. She preferred to be silent and not excuse herself. There was no merit here but natural virtue. What a shame that this good inspiration has vanished!

Oh! everything truly smiled upon me on this earth: I found flowers under each of my steps and my happy disposition contributed much to making life pleasant, but a new period was about to commence for my soul. I had to pass through the crucible of trial and to suffer from my childhood in order to be offered earlier to Jesus. Just as the flowers of spring begin to grow under the snow and to expand in the first rays of the sun, so the little flower whose memories I am writing had to pass through the winter of trial.   — SS 29–30

MAMA'S DEPARTURE

Thérèse's mother died on August 28, 1877. This marked the commencement of the second period of Thérèse's life — a time frequently marked by inner struggle and unhappiness, much of it hidden from those around her.

The day of Mama's departure or the day after, Papa took me in his arms and said: "Come, kiss your poor little Mother for the last time." Without a word I placed my lips on her forehead. I don't recall having cried very much, neither did I speak to anyone about the feelings I experienced. I looked and listened in silence. No one had any time to pay any attention to me, and I saw many things they would have hidden from me. For instance, once I was standing before the lid of the coffin which had been placed upright in the hall. I stopped for a long time gazing at it. Though I'd never seen one before, I understood what it was. I was so little that in spite of Mama's small stature, I had to *raise* my head to take in its full height. It appeared *large* and *dismal....*

The day the Church blessed the mortal remains of our dear Mother, now in heaven, God willed to give me another mother on earth. He willed also that I choose her freely. All five of us were gathered together, looking at each other sadly. Louise was there too, and, seeing Céline and me, she said: "Poor little things, you have no mother any more!" Céline threw her arms around Marie saying: "Well, you will be my Mama!" Accustomed to following Céline's example, I turned instead to you, Mother, and as though the future had torn aside its veil, I threw myself into your arms, crying: "Well, as for me, it's Pauline who will be my Mama!"

As I've already said, it's from the end of this phase in my life that I entered the second period of my existence, the most painful of the three, especially since the entrance into Carmel of the one whom I chose as my second "Mama." This period extends from the age of four and a half to that of fourteen, the time when I found once again my *childhood* character, and entered more and more into the serious side of life. —SS 33–35

A VISION OF FUTURE TRIALS

Thérèse and her father had a very deep emotional bond, and all the more so after the death of her mother. Father and daughter often referred to each other affectionately as "my little Queen" and "my King." In later years Thérèse interpreted the strange incident recounted here, which occurred when she was about six or seven years old, as a foreshadowing of the suffering her father would later undergo as a result of early dementia. In the vision of his veiled face and stooped, burdened body, she

came to recognize a parallel to the typical image of the veiled,
careworn Holy Face of Jesus.

Ah! how joyous were these family feasts! How far I was then
from foreseeing the trials awaiting my dear King when seeing
him so happy! One day, however, God showed me in a truly
extraordinary *vision* the *living* image of the trial He was pleased
to prepare for us in advance.

Papa was on a trip for several days and was not expected
to return for two more days. It could have been about two or
three o'clock in the afternoon; the sun was shining brightly and
all nature seemed to be rejoicing. I was all alone at the window of an attic which faced the large garden; I was looking
straight ahead, my mind occupied with joyful thoughts, when
I saw a man dressed exactly like Papa standing in front of the
laundry which was just opposite. The man had the same height
and walk as Papa, only he was *much more stooped*. His *head*
was covered with a sort of apron of indistinct color and it hid
his face. He wore a hat similar to Papa's. I saw him walking at
a regular pace along my little garden. Immediately a feeling of
supernatural fright invaded my soul, but in an instant I reflected
that surely Papa had returned and was hiding to surprise me;
then I called out very loudly: "Papa! Papa!," my voice trembling
with emotion. But the mysterious personage, appearing not to
hear, continued his steady pace without even turning around.
Following him with my eyes, I saw him go towards the grove
which divides the wide path in two, and I waited to see him
reappear on the other side of the tall trees, but the prophetic
vision had vanished! All this lasted but an instant but was en-
graved so deeply on my heart that today, after fifteen years, it is
as present to me as though I were still seeing the vision before
my eyes.

Marie was with you, Mother, in a room adjoining the one
where I was; hearing me call Papa, she experienced fright also,
feeling, as she told me later, that something extraordinary must
have happened. Without allowing me to see her emotion, she

ran to me and asked what possessed me to call Papa, who was still at Alençon. I told her what I had just seen. To calm me down, Marie said it was no doubt Victoire who hid her head in her apron to frighten me, but when asked about it, Victoire said she hadn't left her kitchen. Besides, I was very sure I'd seen a man and this man had Papa's appearance. Then all three of us went behind the screen of trees, but when we found no mark indicating the passage of anyone, you told me to think no more about it.

It was not within my power to think no more about it. Very often my imagination presented again the mysterious scene I had witnessed. Very often, too, I tried to lift the veil which was hiding its meaning from me because I kept in the bottom of my heart the conviction that this vision had a meaning which was one day to be revealed to me. That day was a long time in coming; but after fourteen years God Himself tore away the mysterious veil.

I had permission to be with Sister Marie of the Sacred Heart, and we were talking as always about the things of the other life and our childhood memories. I recalled to her the vision I had seen at the age of six or seven, and all of a sudden, while I was describing the details of the strange scene, we understood simultaneously what it meant. It was indeed *Papa* whom I had seen advancing, bent over with age. It was indeed Papa, who was bearing on his venerable countenance and white hair the symbol of his *glorious* trial. Just as the adorable Face of Jesus was veiled during His Passion, so the face of His faithful servant had to be veiled in the days of his sufferings in order that it might shine in the heavenly Fatherland near its Lord, the Eternal Word!

It is from the midst of this ineffable glory where he reigns in heaven that our dear Father obtained for us the grace to understand the vision his little Queen had at an age when illusions are not to be feared. It is from the midst of glory he obtained this sweet consolation of understanding that God, ten years before our great trial, was already showing it to us. He was doing this as a Father who gives His children a glimpse of the glorious future He is preparing for them and is pleased to have them consider in advance the priceless riches which will be their heritage.

Ah! why was it to me that God gave this light? Why did He show such a small child a thing she couldn't understand, a thing which, if she had understood, would have made her die of grief. Why? This is one of the mysteries we shall understand only in heaven and which we shall eternally admire!   — SS 45–47

THE VIRGIN OF THE SMILE

In October of 1882, Thérèse's big sister and "second mama" Pauline, entered Carmel. At the same time, nine-year-old Thérèse returned to school at the Benedictine Abbey. Both of these were traumatic events for her. Before long, she began to manifest signs of illness. There has been much debate over the balance among physiological, psychological, and spiritual sources of this illness. The bottom line, in any case, is the moment of healing grace Thérèse experienced through the mediation of a statue of an open-armed, gently smiling Virgin Mary. This statue was later moved to Lisieux Carmel, and it is still often seen represented on holy cards honoring St. Thérèse.

Towards the end of the year, I began to have a constant headache. It didn't cause me much suffering. I was able to pursue my studies and nobody was worried about me. This lasted until Easter, 1883. Papa had gone to Paris with Marie and Léonie, and Aunt had taken me and Céline with her into her home. One evening Uncle took me for a walk and spoke about Mama and about past memories with a kindness that touched me profoundly and made me cry. Then he told me I was too softhearted, that I needed a lot of distraction, and he was determined to give us a good time during our Easter vacation. He and Aunt would see to it. That night we were to go to the

Catholic Circle meeting, but finding I was too fatigued, Aunt made me go to bed; when I was undressing, I was seized with a strange trembling. Believing I was cold, Aunt covered me with blankets and surrounded me with hot water bottles. But nothing was able to stop my shaking which lasted almost all night. Uncle, returning from the meeting with my cousins and Céline, was very much surprised to see me in this state which he judged to be very serious. He didn't want to say this in order not to frighten Aunt.

He went to get Doctor Notta the next day, and he judged, as did Uncle, that I had a very serious illness and one which had never before attacked a child as young as I. Everybody was puzzled. Aunt was obliged to keep me at her home, and she took care of me with a truly *maternal* solicitude. When Papa returned from Paris with my older sisters, Aimée met them at the door with such a sad face that Marie believed I had died. This sickness was not "unto death," but like that of Lazarus it was to give glory to God. And God was glorified by the admirable resignation of my poor little *Father,* who thought his *"little girl was going crazy or was about to die."* ...

We were at the time in the beautiful month of May, and nature was adorned with flowers and was bursting out with joy. The *"little flower"* alone was languishing and seemed forever withered.

However, she had a Sun near her, and this Sun was the *miraculous statue* of the Blessed Virgin which had spoken to Mama twice, and the little flower, often, very often, turned her petals toward this blessed Star. One day I saw Papa enter Marie's room where I was in bed. He gave her several pieces of gold with an expression of great sadness and told her to write to Paris and have some Masses said at Our Lady of Victories so that she would cure his poor little girl. Ah! how touched I was to see my dear King's faith and love! I would have loved to be able to tell him I was cured; but I had already given him enough false joys, and it wasn't my desires which could work a *miracle,* and a miracle was necessary for my cure.

A miracle was necessary and it was our Lady of Victories who worked it. One Sunday during the Novena of Masses, Marie went into the garden, leaving me with Léonie who was reading near the window. After a few moments I began calling in a low tone: "Mama, Mama." Léonie, accustomed to hearing me always calling out like this, didn't pay any attention. This lasted a long time, and then I called her much louder. Marie finally returned. I saw her enter, but I cannot say I recognized her and continued to call her in a louder tone: "Mama." *I was suffering very much* from this forced and inexplicable struggle and Marie was suffering perhaps even more than I. After some futile attempts to show me she was by my side, Marie knelt down near my bed with Léonie and Céline. Turning to the Blessed Virgin and praying with the fervor of a mother begging for the life of her child, *Marie* obtained what she wanted.

Finding no help on earth, poor little Thérèse had also turned towards the Mother of heaven, and prayed with all her heart that she take pity on her. All of a sudden the Blessed Virgin appeared beautiful to me, so *beautiful* that never had I seen anything so attractive; her face was suffused with an ineffable benevolence and tenderness, but what penetrated to the very depths of my soul was the *"ravishing smile of the Blessed Virgin."* At that instant, all my pains disappeared, and two large tears glistened on my eyelashes, and flowed down my cheeks silently, but they were tears of unmixed joy. Ah! I thought, the Blessed Virgin smiled at me, how happy I am, but never will I tell anyone for my *happiness would then disappear*. Without any effort I lowered my eyes, and I saw Marie who was looking down at me lovingly; she seemed moved and appeared to surmise the favor the Blessed Virgin had given me. Ah! it was really to her, to her touching prayers that I owed the grace of the Queen of heaven's *smile*. Seeing my gaze fixed on the Blessed Virgin, she cried out: "Thérèse is cured!" Yes, the little flower was going to be born again to life, and the luminous Ray that had warmed her again was not to stop its favors; the Ray did not act all at once, but sweetly and gently it raised the little flower and strengthened her in such a way that five years later she was expanding on the fertile mountain of Carmel.

— SS 60–61; 64–66

FIRST COMMUNION

In France at that time, the sacraments of First Eucharist and Confirmation were typically received around age eleven or twelve. Eleven-year-old Thérèse celebrated her First Communion on May 8, 1884, and her Confirmation on June 14 of the same year. For her, these were genuine events of conversion; even at this early age, she had a profound awareness of the reality and implications of interior union with Jesus.

The "beautiful day of days" finally arrived. The *smallest details* of that heavenly day have left unspeakable memories in my soul! The joyous awakening at dawn, the *respectful* embraces of the teachers and our older companions! The large room filled with *snow-white* dresses in which each child was to be clothed in her turn! Above all, the procession into the chapel and the singing of the *morning* hymn: "O altar of God, where the angels are hovering!"

I don't want to enter into detail here. There are certain things that lose their perfume as soon as they are exposed to the air; there are deep *spiritual thoughts* which cannot be expressed in human language without losing their intimate and heavenly meaning; they are similar to " ... *the white stone I will give to him who conquers, with a name written on the stone which no one KNOWS except HIM who receives it*" [Rev. 2:17].

Ah! how sweet was that first kiss of Jesus! It was a kiss of *love;* I *felt* that I *was loved,* and I said: "I love You, and I give myself to You forever!" There were no demands made, no struggles, no sacrifices; for a long time now Jesus and poor little Thérèse *looked at* and understood each other. That day, it was no longer simply a *look,* it was a fusion; they were no

longer two, Thérèse had vanished as a drop of water is lost in
the immensity of the ocean. Jesus alone remained; He was the
Master, the King. Had not Thérèse asked Him to take away her
liberty, for her *liberty* frightened her? She felt so feeble and fragile that she wanted to be united forever to the divine Strength!
Her joy was too great, too deep for her to contain, and tears of
consolation soon flowed, to the great consternation of her companions. They asked one another: "Why was she crying? Was
there something bothering her?" — "No, it was because her
mother was not there or her sister whom she loves so much, her
sister the Carmelite." They did not understand that all the joy
of Heaven having entered my heart, this exiled heart was unable
to bear it without shedding tears. Oh! no, the absence of Mama
didn't cause me any sorrow on the day of my First Communion. Wasn't Heaven itself in my soul, and hadn't Mama taken
her place there a long time ago? Thus in receiving Jesus' visit, I
received also Mama's. She blessed me and rejoiced at my happiness. I was not crying because of Pauline's absence. I would
have been happy to see her by my side, but for a long time
I had accepted my sacrifice of her. On that day, joy alone filled
my heart and I united myself to her who gave herself irrevocably
to Him who gave Himself so lovingly to me!

In the afternoon, it was I who made the Act of Consecration
to the Blessed Virgin. It was only right that I *speak* in the name
of my companions to my Mother in heaven, I who had been
deprived at such an early age of my earthly Mother. I put all
my heart into *speaking* to her, into consecrating myself to her
as a child throwing itself into the arms of its mother, asking her
to watch over her. It seems to me the Blessed Virgin must have
looked upon her little flower and *smiled* at her, for wasn't it she
who cured her with a *visible smile*? Had she not placed in the
heart of her little flower her Jesus, the Flower of the Fields and
the Lily of the valley?

In the evening of that beautiful day, I found myself once more
with my family. Already in the morning at the Mass, I had embraced *Papa* and all my relatives. But now this was the real

reunion and Papa took the hand of his little Queen and brought her to *Carmel*. There I saw my *Pauline* who had become the spouse of Jesus; I saw her with her white veil, one like mine, and her crown of roses. Ah! my joy was without bitterness. I hoped to be with her soon and to await *heaven* with her! I was not indifferent to the family feast which took place the night of my First Communion. The beautiful watch my King gave me was the cause of great pleasure, but my joy was tranquil and nothing came to disturb my interior peace. Marie took me with her into her room on the night which followed this beautiful day, for the most brilliant days are followed by darkness; only the day of the first, the unique, the eternal Communion of heaven will be endless!

The day after my First Communion was still beautiful, but it was tinged with a certain melancholy. The beautiful dress Marie had bought me, all the gifts I had received did not satisfy my heart. Jesus only could do this, and I longed for the moment when I could receive Him a second time. About a month after my First Communion, I went to confession for the Ascension and I dared ask permission to receive Holy Communion. Against all hope, the priest permitted it and so I had the happiness of kneeling at the communion railing between Papa and Marie. What a sweet memory I have of this second visit of Jesus! My tears flowed again with an ineffable sweetness, and I repeated to myself these words of St. Paul: "It is no longer I that live, it is Jesus who lives in me!" Since that Communion, my desire to receive grew more and more, and I obtained permission to go to Holy Communion on all the principal feasts. On the eve of each of these happy days, Marie took me on her knees and prepared me as she did for my First Communion. I remember how once she was speaking to me about suffering and she told me that I would probably not walk that way, that God would always carry me as a child.

The day after my Communion, the words of Marie came to my mind. I felt born within my heart a *great desire* to suffer, and at the same time the interior assurance that Jesus reserved a great number of crosses for me. I felt myself flooded with consolations so *great* that I look upon them as one of the *greatest* graces of my life. Suffering became my attraction; it had charms about it which ravished me without my understanding them very well. Up until this time, I had suffered without *loving* suffering, but since this day I felt a real love for it. I also felt the desire of loving only God, of finding my joy only in Him. Often during my Communions, I repeated these words of the *Imitation*: "O Jesus, unspeakable *sweetness*, change all the consolations of this earth into *bitterness* for me." This prayer fell from my lips without effort, without constraint; it seemed I repeated it not with my will but like a child who repeats the words a person he loves has inspired in him. Later I will tell you, dear Mother, how Jesus was pleased to realize my desire, and how He was always my ineffable *sweetness*.   — SS 77–80

THE GRACE OF CHRISTMAS

According to her own testimony, Thérèse left her childhood behind on Christmas Eve, 1886. The story of her "Christmas conversion" is a classic example of how the smallest and most ordinary affairs of human life, attended to on the level of soul-narrative, may truly become events of the manifestation of God. The third period of Thérèse's life was beginning.

Although God showered His graces upon me, it wasn't because I merited them because I was still very imperfect. I had a great desire, it is true, to practice virtue, but I went about it in a strange way. Being the youngest in the family, I wasn't accustomed to doing things for myself. Céline tidied up the room in which we slept, and I myself didn't do any housework whatsoever. After Marie's entrance into Carmel, it sometimes happened that I tried to make up the bed to please God, or else in the evening, when Céline was away, I'd bring in her plants. But as I already said, it was for *God alone* I was doing these things and should not have expected any *thanks* from creatures. Alas, it was just the opposite. If Céline was unfortunate enough not to seem happy or surprised because of these little services, I became unhappy and proved it by my tears.

I was really unbearable because of my extreme touchiness; if I happened to cause anyone I loved some little trouble, even unwittingly, instead of forgetting about it and not *crying*, which made matters worse, I cried like a Magdalene and then when I began to cheer up, I'd begin *to cry again for having cried*. All arguments were useless; I was quite unable to correct this terrible fault. I really don't know how I could entertain the thought of entering Carmel when I was still in the *swaddling clothes of a child!*

God would have to work a little miracle to make me *grow up* in an instant, and this miracle He performed on that unforgettable Christmas day. On that luminous *night* which sheds such light on the delights of the Holy Trinity, Jesus, the gentle, *little* Child of only one hour, changed the night of my soul into rays of light. On that *night* when He made Himself subject to *weakness* and suffering for love of me, He made me *strong* and courageous, arming me with His weapons. Since that night I have never been defeated in any combat, but rather walked from victory to victory, beginning, so to speak, *"to run as a giant"!* [Psalm 18:6]. The source of my tears was dried up and has since re-opened rarely and with great difficulty. This justified what was often said to me: "You cry so much during your childhood, you'll no longer have tears to shed later on!"

It was December 25, 1886, that I received the grace of leaving my childhood, in a word, the grace of my complete conversion. We had come back from Midnight Mass where I had the happiness of receiving the strong and *powerful* God. Upon arriving at Les Buissonnets, I used to love to take my shoes from the chimney-corner and examine the presents in them; this old custom had given us so much joy in our youth that Céline wanted to continue treating me as a baby since I was the youngest in the family. Papa had always loved to see my happiness and listen to my cries of delight as I drew each surprise from the *magic shoes,* and my dear King's gaiety increased my own happiness very much. However, Jesus desired to show me that I was to give up the defects of my childhood and so He withdrew its innocent pleasures. He permitted Papa, tired out after the Midnight Mass, to experience annoyance when seeing my shoes at the fireplace, and that he speak those words which pierced my heart: "Well, fortunately, this will be the last year!" I was going upstairs, at the time, to remove my hat, and Céline, knowing how sensitive I was and seeing the tears already glistening in my eyes, wanted to cry too, for she loved me very much and understood my grief. She said, "Oh, Thérèse, don't go downstairs; it would cause you too much grief to look at your slippers right now!" But Thérèse was no longer the same; Jesus had changed her heart! Forcing back my tears, I descended the stairs rapidly; controlling the poundings of my heart, I took my slippers and placed them in front of Papa, and withdrew all the objects joyfully. I had the happy appearance of a Queen. Having regained his own cheerfulness, Papa was laughing; Céline believed it was all a *dream!* Fortunately, it was a sweet reality; Thérèse had discovered once again the strength of soul which she had lost at the age of four and a half, and she was to preserve it forever!

On that *night of light* began the third period of my life, the most beautiful and the most filled with graces from heaven. The work I had been unable to do in ten years was done by Jesus in one instant, contenting himself with my *good will* which was never lacking. I could say to Him like His apostles: "Master, I fished all night and caught nothing." More merciful to me than He was to His disciples, Jesus *took the net Himself,* cast it, and drew it in filled with fish. He made me a fisher of *souls.* I experienced a great desire to work for the conversion of sinners, a desire I hadn't felt so intensely before.

I felt *charity* enter into my soul, and the need to forget myself and to please others; since then I've been happy!   — SS 97–99

THIRST FOR SOULS

Immediately after her Christmas conversion, Thérèse found herself deeply drawn to prayer for sinners. The spirituality of the time often focused on rather maudlin images of the suffering and wounds of Jesus; but Thérèse found her way straight to the heart of the matter, recognizing Jesus' wounds as a pouring forth of infinite mercy and compassion from the Heart of God. She saw an unmistakable confirmation of her vocation in the remarkable response to her prayer for the notorious murderer Henri Pranzini, whose execution took place on August 31, 1887.

One Sunday, looking at a picture of Our Lord on the Cross, I was struck by the blood flowing from one of the divine hands. I felt a great pang of sorrow when thinking this blood was falling to the ground without anyone's hastening to gather it up. I was resolved to remain in spirit at the foot of the Cross and to receive the divine dew. I understood I was then to pour it out upon souls. The cry of Jesus on the Cross sounded continually in my heart: *"I thirst!"* These words ignited within me an unknown and very living fire. I wanted to give my Beloved to drink and I felt myself consumed with a *thirst for souls*. As yet, it was not the souls of priests that attracted me, but those of *great sinners*; I *burned* with the desire to snatch them from the eternal flames.

To awaken my zeal God showed me my desires were pleasing to Him. I heard talk of a great criminal just condemned to death for some horrible crimes; everything pointed to the fact that he would die impenitent. I wanted at all costs to prevent him from falling into hell, and to attain my purpose I employed every means imaginable. Feeling that of myself I could do nothing, I offered to God all the infinite merits of Our Lord, the treasures of the Church, and finally I begged Céline to have a Mass offered for my intentions. I didn't dare ask this myself for fear of being obliged to say it was for Pranzini, the great criminal.

I didn't even want to tell Céline, but she asked me such tender and pressing questions, I confided my secret to her. Far from laughing at me, she asked if she could help convert *my sinner*. I accepted gratefully, for I would have wished all creatures would unite with me to beg grace for the guilty man.

I felt in the depths of my heart *certain* that our desires would be granted, but to obtain courage to pray for sinners I told God I was sure He would pardon the poor, unfortunate Pranzini; that I'd believe this even if he went to his death without *any signs of repentance* or without *having gone to confession*. I was absolutely confident in the mercy of Jesus. But I was begging Him for a *"sign"* of repentance only for my own simple consolation.

My prayer was answered to the letter! In spite of Papa's prohibition that we read no papers, I didn't think I was disobeying when reading the passages pertaining to Pranzini. The day after his execution I found the newspaper *"La Croix."* I opened it quickly and what did I see? Ah! my tears betrayed my emotion and I was obliged to hide. Pranzini had not gone to confession. He had mounted the scaffold and was preparing to place his head in the formidable opening, when suddenly, seized by an inspiration, he turned, took hold of the *crucifix* the priest was holding out to him and *kissed* the *sacred wounds three times!* Then his soul went to receive the *merciful* sentence of Him who declares that in heaven there will be more joy over one sinner who does penance then over ninety-nine just who have no need of repentance!

I had obtained the "sign" I requested, and this sign was a perfect replica of the grace Jesus had given me when He attracted me to pray for sinners. Wasn't it before the *wounds of Jesus,* when seeing His divine *blood* flowing, that the thirst for souls had entered my heart? I wished to give them this *immaculate blood* to drink, this blood which was to purify them from their stains, and the lips of my *"first child"* were pressed to the sacred wounds!

What an unspeakably sweet response! After this unique grace my desire to save souls grows each day, and I seemed to hear Jesus say to me what he said to the Samaritan woman: *"Give me to drink!"* It was a true interchange of love: to souls I was giving the *blood of Jesus,* to Jesus I was offering these same souls refreshed by the *divine dew.* I slaked His thirst and the more I gave Him *to drink,* the more the thirst of my poor little soul increased, and it was this ardent thirst He was giving me as the most delightful drink of His love.   — SS 99–101

AUDIENCE WITH THE POPE

On Pentecost Sunday of 1887, fourteen-year-old Thérèse had asked for and received her beloved father's permission to enter Lisieux Carmel. Because she was far younger than the normal age of entrance, and because two of her elder siblings (Pauline and Marie) were already in the same Carmel, she also needed special permission from Church officials. Summarily turned down by both the priest in charge of the Carmel and the local bishop, Thérèse refused to give up her quest. With her father and her sister Céline, she joined a pilgrimage to holy sites in France and Italy. The tour included several days in Rome as well as an audience with Pope Leo XIII. During the audience, Thérèse took her case straight to the top.

Sunday, November 20, after dressing up according to Vatican regulations, i.e., in black with a lace mantilla as head-piece, and decorated with a large medal of Leo XIII, tied with a blue and white ribbon, we entered the Vatican through the Sovereign Pontiff's chapel. At eight o'clock in the morning our emotion was profound when we saw him enter to celebrate Holy Mass. After blessing the numerous pilgrims gathered round him, he climbed the steps of the altar and showed us through his piety, worthy of the Vicar of Jesus, that he was truly "the *Holy*

Father." My heart beat strongly and my prayers were fervent
when Jesus descended into the hands of His Pontiff. However, I
was filled with confidence, for the Gospel of the day contained
these beautiful words: "Fear not, little flock, for it is your Father's good pleasure to give you the kingdom" [Luke 12:32].
No, I did not fear, I hoped the kingdom of Carmel would soon
belong to me; I was not thinking then of those other words of
Jesus: "And I appoint to you a kingdom even as my Father has
appointed to me..." [Luke 22:29]. In other words, I reserve
crosses and trials for you, and it is thus you will be worthy of
possessing this kingdom after which you long; since it was necessary that the Christ suffer and that He enter through it into
His glory, if you desire to have a place by His side, then drink
the chalice He has drunk! This chalice was presented to me by
the Holy Father and my tears mingled with the bitter potion I
was offered.

After the Mass of thanksgiving, following that of the Holy
Father, the audience began. Leo XIII was seated on a large arm-
chair; he was dressed simply in a white cassock, with a cape of
the same color, and on his head was a little skullcap. Around
him were cardinals, archbishops, and bishops, but I saw them
only in general, being occupied solely with the Holy Father. We
passed in front of him in procession; each pilgrim knelt in turn,
kissed the foot and hand of Leo XIII, received his blessing, and
two noble guards touched him as a sign to rise (touched the
pilgrim, for I explain myself so badly one would think it was
the Pope).

Before entering the pontifical apartment, I was really determined *to speak,* but I felt my courage weaken when I saw
Father Reverony standing by the Holy Father's right side. Almost at the same instant, they told us on the Pope's *behalf*
that *it was forbidden to speak,* as this would prolong the audience too much. I turned towards my dear Céline for advice:
"Speak!," she said. A moment later I was at the Holy Father's
feet. I kissed his slipper and he presented his hand, but instead

of kissing it I joined my own and lifting tear-filled eyes to his face, I cried out: "Most Holy Father, I have a great favor to ask you!"

The Sovereign Pontiff lowered his head towards me in such a way that my face almost touched his, and I saw his eyes, black and deep, fixed on me and they seemed to penetrate to the depths of my soul. "Holy Father, in honor of your Jubilee, permit me to enter Carmel at the age of fifteen!"

Emotion undoubtedly made my voice tremble. He turned to Father Reverony who was staring at me with surprise and displeasure and said: "I don't understand very well." Now if God had permitted it, it would have been easy for Father Reverony to obtain what I desired, but it was the cross and not consolation God willed to give me.

"Most Holy Father," answered the Vicar General, "this is *a child* who wants to enter Carmel at the age of fifteen, but the Superiors are considering the matter at the moment." "Well, my child," the Holy Father replied, looking at me kindly, "do what the Superiors tell you!" Resting my hands on his knees, I made a final effort, saying in a suppliant voice: "Oh! Holy Father, if you say yes, everybody will agree!" He gazed at me steadily, speaking these words and stressing each syllable: "Go...go... *You will enter if God wills it!*" (His accent had something about it so penetrating and so convincing, it seems to me I still hear it.)

I was encouraged by the Holy Father's kindness and wanted to speak again, but the two guards *touched* me *politely* to make me rise. As this was not enough they took me by the arms and Father Reverony helped them lift me, for I stayed there with joined hands resting on the knees of Leo XIII. It was with *force* they dragged me from his feet. At the moment I was *thus lifted*, the Holy Father placed his hand on my lips, then raised it to bless me. Then my eyes filled with tears and Father Reverony was able to contemplate at least as many *diamonds* as he had seen at Bayeux. The two guards literally carried me to the door and there a third one gave me a medal of Leo XIII....

At the termination of the audience, my dear Father was grieved to find me in tears. He did his best to console me but without success. In the bottom of my heart I felt a great peace, since I had done everything in my power to answer what God was asking of me. This *peace,* however, was in the *depths* only; bitterness *filled* my soul, for Jesus was silent. He seemed to be absent, nothing served to reveal His presence. That day, too, the sun dared not shine and Italy's beautiful blue skies, covered with dark clouds, never stopped crying with me. Ah! it was all over; my trip no longer held any attraction for me since its purpose had failed. The final words of the Pontiff should have consoled me, for were they not a real prophecy? *In spite of* all obstacles, what *God willed* was really accomplished. *He did not allow* creatures to do what they willed but *what He willed.*

I had offered myself, for some time now, to the Child Jesus as His *little plaything.* I told Him not to use me as a valuable toy children are content to look at but dare not touch, but to use me like a little ball of no value which He could throw on the ground, push with His foot, *pierce,* leave in a corner, or press to His heart if it pleased Him; in a word, I wanted to *amuse little Jesus,* to give Him pleasure; I wanted to give myself up to His *childish whims.* He heard my prayer.

At Rome, Jesus pierced His little plaything; He wanted to see what there was inside it and having seen, content with His discovery, He let His little ball fall to the ground and He went off to sleep. What did He do during His gentle sleep and what became of the little abandoned ball? Jesus dreamed *He was still playing* with His toy, leaving it and taking it up in turns, and then having seen it roll quite far He pressed it to His heart, no longer allowing it to ever go far from His little hand.

You understand, dear Mother, how sad the little ball was when seeing itself on the ground. Nevertheless, I never ceased hoping against all hope.   — SS 133–36

ENTRANCE TO CARMEL

Thérèse's grief turned to joy about a month later, when the local bishop reversed his previous decision and gave his permission for her to enter Lisieux Carmel. She was greatly disappointed, however, by his requirement that she wait until after the community's rigorous Lenten fast was completed. She was still only fifteen when she became a Carmelite postulant.

The day chosen for my entrance into Carmel was April 9, 1888, the same day the community was celebrating the feast of the Annunciation, transferred because of Lent. The evening before, the whole family gathered round the table where I was to sit for the last time. Ah! how heartrending these family reunions can really be! When you would like to see yourself forgotten, the most tender caresses and words are showered upon you making the sacrifice of separation felt all the more.

Papa was not saying very much, but his gaze was fixed upon me lovingly. Aunt cried from time to time and Uncle paid me many affectionate compliments. Jeanne and Marie gave me all sorts of little attentions, especially Marie, who, taking me aside, asked pardon for the troubles she thought she caused me. My dear little Léonie, who had returned from the Visitation a few months previously, kissed and embraced me often. There is only Céline, about whom I have not spoken, but you can well imagine, dear Mother, how we spent that last night together.

On the morning of the great day, casting a last look upon Les Buissonnets, that beautiful cradle of my childhood which I was never to see again, I left on my dear King's arm to climb Mount Carmel. As on the evening before, the whole family was reunited to hear Holy Mass and receive Communion. As soon as Jesus descended into the hearts of my relatives, I heard nothing around me but sobs. I was the only one who didn't shed any tears, but my heart was beating *so violently* it seemed impossible to walk when they signaled for me to come to the enclosure door. I advanced, however, asking myself whether I was going

to die because of the beating of my heart! Ah! what a moment
that was! One would have to experience it to know what it is.

My emotion was not noticed exteriorly. After embracing all
the members of the family, I knelt down before my matchless
Father for his blessing, and to give it to me he placed *himself
on his knees* and blessed me, tears flowing down his cheeks. It
was a spectacle to make the angels smile, this spectacle of an
old man presenting his child, still in the springtime of life, to
the Lord! A few moments later, the doors of the holy ark closed
upon me, and there I was received by the *dear Sisters* who embraced me. They had acted as mothers to me and I was going to
take them as models for my actions from now on. My desires
were at last accomplished; my soul experienced a *PEACE* so
sweet, so deep, it would be impossible to express it. For seven
years and a half that inner peace has remained my lot, and has
not abandoned me in the midst of the greatest trials.

I was led, as are all postulants, to the choir immediately after
my entrance into the cloister. The choir was in darkness because
the Blessed Sacrament was exposed and what struck me first
were the eyes of our holy Mother Genevieve which were fixed
on me. I remained kneeling for a moment at her feet, thanking
God for the grace He gave me of knowing a saint, and then I
followed Mother Marie de Gonzague into the different places
of the community. Everything thrilled me; I felt as though I was
transported into a desert; our little cell, above all, filled me with
joy. But the joy I was experiencing was *calm,* the lightest breeze
did not undulate the quiet waters upon which my little boat was
floating and no cloud darkened my blue heaven. Ah! I was fully
recompensed for all my trials. With what deep joy I repeated
those words: "I am here forever and ever!"

This happiness was not passing. It didn't take its flight with
"the illusions of the first days." *Illusions,* God gave me the
grace *not to have A SINGLE ONE* when entering Carmel. I
found the religious life to be *exactly* as I had imagined it, no
sacrifice astonished me and yet, as you know, dear Mother,
my first steps met with more thorns than roses! Yes, suffering

opened wide its arms to me and I threw myself into them with love. I had declared at the feet of Jesus-Victim, in the examination preceding my Profession, what I had come to Carmel for: "I came to save souls and especially to pray for priests." When one wishes to attain a goal, one must use the means; Jesus made me understand that it was through suffering that He wanted to give me souls, and my attraction for suffering grew in proportion to its increase. This was my way for five years; exteriorly nothing revealed my suffering which was all the more painful since I alone was aware of it. Ah! what a surprise we shall have at the end of the world when we shall read the story of souls! There will be those who will be surprised when they see the way through which my soul was guided!   — SS 147–49

2

Thérèse,
Best Friend and Sister

Even though they were a full three years apart in age, Thérèse and her sister Céline had from childhood shared an intimate soul-bond that deeply sustained and delighted both of them. When Thérèse joined their two oldest sisters in Lisieux Carmel in 1888, Céline found herself required to remain home to take responsibility for their ill father. The letters that Thérèse wrote to Céline during the years before Céline herself entered Lisieux Carmel in September 1894 offer some of the most detailed and strikingly poetic expressions of Thérèse's developing spirituality.

The letters selected were written when Thérèse was between eighteen and twenty-one years old. Composed during the years just preceding the writing of Story of a Soul, *they reveal Thérèse as a vital young nun who was hard at work soaking up wisdom, refining it in the meditations of her heart, and learning how to offer it in charming form to others.* Story of a Soul *says very little about these years, but it is clear that they laid a strong foundation for what was to come. It is worth quoting in full a sketch of Thérèse from a letter sent by one of the other nuns at about the midpoint of this period:*

> *Thérèse of the Child Jesus, twenty years old. Novice and jewel of the Carmel, its dear Benjamin. Office of painting*

in which she excels without having had any other lessons than those of seeing our Reverend Mother, her dear sister, at work. Tall and strong, with the appearance of a child, a tone of voice, an expression, hiding within her a wisdom, a perfection, a perspicacity of a fifty-year-old. Soul always calm and in perfect possession of itself in all things and with everybody. Little innocent thing, to whom one would give God without confession, but whose head is full of mischief to play on anyone she pleases. Mystic, comic, everything.... She can make you weep with devotion and just as easily split your sides with laughter during our recreations. (LT vol. 2, p. 778)

These were very difficult years for Céline, and Thérèse's letters clearly manifest the profound care and solicitude she felt for her struggling "soul sister." Now offered to the wider community of Christians, they can extend their gifts of sage advice and consoling support to all who are enduring great burdens and trials.

JESUS' LITTLE CÉLINE-FLOWER

As she wrote for Céline's feast day (October 21), Thérèse was fresh from a community retreat that she later said "launched me full sail upon the waves of confidence and love" [SS 174]. Here Thérèse expands upon the unity of soul she feels with Céline and tenderly affirms that Céline too is a "little flower." She plays upon the fact that "Céline" is also the name of a type of aster, which apparently had bloomed early that year despite the unusually rugged winter. The specific suffering Céline was undergoing at this time was probably the burden of making demanding but largely unappreciated visits to their father in the nursing home at Caen. Some namecalling and minor violence had recently broken out between Catholics and anticlericals; this may lie behind the allusion to martyrdom.

October 20, 1891

Dear Céline,

This is the fourth time I am coming to wish you a happy feast since I am in Carmel....

It seems to me that these four years have tightened even more the bonds that united us so closely. The more we advance the more we love Jesus, and as it is in Him that we cherish each other, this is why our affection becomes so strong that it is rather *unity* than union which exists between our two souls!... Yes, but I want to tell you why the *Célines* have blossomed earlier this year. Jesus made me feel it this morning for your feast. You have undoubtedly noticed that never had winter been so rigorous as last year, consequently, all flowers were retarded in their blossoming. This was very natural, and no one dreamed of being astonished by it. But there is a little mysterious flower that Jesus has reserved for Himself in order to instruct our souls. This flower is the Céline-flower... contrary to the other flowers, it blossomed one month before the time of its blossoming.... Céline, do you understand the language of my dear little flower... the flower of my childhood... the flower of our memories?!!!!... Wintry weather, the rigors of winter, instead of retarding it, made it grow and blossom.... No one paid any attention to it; this flower is so little, so unattractive... only the bees know the treasures that its mysterious calyx encloses, made up of a multitude of little calyxes, each one as rich as the others.... Thérèse, like the bees, understood this mystery. Winter is suffering; suffering misunderstood, misjudged, looked upon as useless by profane eyes, but as fruitful and powerful in the eyes of Jesus and the angels who, like the vigilant bees, know how to gather the honey contained within the mysterious and multiple calyxes that represent souls or rather the children of the virginal little flower.... Céline, I would need volumes to write all I am thinking about my little flower... for me it is so perfect an image of your soul. Yes, Jesus has made wintry weather pass over it instead of the warm sun of His consolations, but the effect expected by Him has been produced; the little plant has grown and has blossomed almost in one act.... Céline, when a flower has blossomed, we have only to pluck it, but when and how will Jesus pluck His little flower?... Perhaps the pink color of its corolla indicates that this will be by means of martyrdom!... Yes, I feel my desires are reborn. Perhaps after having asked us love for love, so to speak, Jesus will want to ask us blood for blood, life for life.... In the meantime, we must let the bees draw out all the honey from the little calyxes, keeping nothing, giving all to Jesus, and then we shall say like the flower in the evening of our life: "The night, behold the night." Then it will be finished.... And to the wintry blasts will succeed the gentle rays of the sun, to the tears of Jesus, eternal smiles....

Ah, let us not refuse to weep with Him during one day since we shall enjoy His glory throughout an eternity!...

Dear little flower, do you understand your Thérèse?...

—LT #132

THE DOUBLE DAISY

Thérèse again expresses her conviction that she and Céline are truly "one flower," destined to be together forever. Thérèse frequently worried that Céline might choose a path different from her own; indeed, there had been a young suitor in the picture, and Céline admitted to having found the vocation of marriage somewhat attractive. This is one of the reasons for Thérèse's frequent emphasis on the importance of keeping one's eyes fixed on "Jesus alone."

April 26, 1892

Dear Céline,

The meadow of Carmel supplies me this year with a symbolic gift that I am happy to offer you for your twenty-three years.... One day, in the grass all-whitened by simple daisies, I seemed to see one of them with a long stem, and it surpassed them in beauty; coming close, I saw with surprise that instead of one daisy there were two very distinct ones. Two stems so tightly joined together put me in mind immediately of the mysteries of *our souls*.... I understood that, if in the order of nature Jesus is pleased to sow beneath our feet marvels so delightful, it is only to aid us in reading into more hidden mysteries of a superior order that He is working at times in souls.... Céline, I feel that you have already understood your Thérèse, already your heart has guessed at what is taking place in this other heart to which yours is so tightly united that the sap nourishing them is the same!... However, I want to speak to you about some of the hidden mysteries in my little flower. Jesus has created a multitude of little daisies to give joy to our eyes and to instruct our souls. I see with surprise that, in the morning, their pink corollas are turned in the direction of the dawn, they are awaiting the rising of the sun; as soon as this radiant star has sent toward them its warm rays, the timid little flowers open up their calyxes, and their dainty leaves form a sort of crown which, uncovering their little yellow hearts, give immediately to these flowers a great resemblance to what has struck them with its light. Throughout the whole day, the daisies do not cease gazing on the sun, and they turn like it until the evening; then when it has disappeared, they quickly close again their corollas, and from white they become pink.... Jesus is the divine Sun, and the daisies are His spouses, the virgins. When Jesus has looked upon a soul, He immediately gives it His divine resemblance, but it is necessary that this soul not cease to fix its eyes upon Him *alone*. To develop the mysteries of daisies, I would have to write a volume; however, my Céline understands all, so now I want to speak to her about the whims of Jesus.... In His meadows, Jesus has many daisies, but they are separated, and they receive the rays of the Sun each one separately. One day, the Spouse of virgins bent down to earth; He united tightly two little buds scarcely open, their stems were merged into a single one, and one look made them grow up. Together these little flowers, *now only one flower,* blossomed, and now the double daisy, fixing its eyes on the divine Sun, accomplishes its mission which is one.... Céline, you alone can understand my language; in the eyes of creatures, our life seems very different, very much separated, but I myself know that Jesus has joined our hearts in so marvelous a way that what makes one heart beat also makes the other heart throb.... "Where your treasure is there is your heart also." Our treasure is Jesus, and our hearts make up only one in Him. The same look ravished our souls, a look veiled in tears, which the double daisy has resolved to dry; its humble and white corolla will be the calyx in which precious diamonds will be collected to be poured out on other flowers that, less privileged, will not have fixed upon Jesus the first glance of their hearts.... Perhaps, in the evening of its life, the daisy will offer the divine Spouse its corolla, become pink.

Adieu, dear Céline, the little flower I am sending you is a relic, for it has rested in the hands of our saintly Mother Genevieve, and she has blessed Céline and Thérèse....

Thérèse of the Child Jesus of the Holy Face
—LT #134

THE APOSTOLATE OF PRAYER

Thérèse added a long note to a letter to Céline written by their sister Pauline (known in Carmel as Sister Agnes). In it she quotes two of her major sources of spiritual nourishment — the gospels and the writings of the Carmelite St. John of the Cross — as she expounds on her growing insight into the crucial role of our cooperation with God on behalf of others.

August 15, 1892

Dear Céline,

I cannot allow the letter to leave without joining a note to it. For this, I must steal a few moments from Jesus, but He does not hold it against me, for it is about Him that we speak together, without Him no discourse has any charms for our

hearts. ... Céline, the vast solitudes, the enchanting horizons
opening up before you must be speaking volumes to your soul?
I myself see nothing of all that, but I say with Saint John of the
Cross: "My Beloved is the mountains, and lonely, wooded valleys, etc." And this Beloved instructs my soul, He speaks to it
in silence, in darkness. ... Recently, there came a thought to me
which I have to tell my Céline. It was one day when I was thinking of what I could do to save souls, a word of the gospel gave
me a real light. In days gone by, Jesus said to His disciples when
showing them the fields of ripe corn: "Lift up your eyes and see
how the fields are already white enough to be harvested," and
a little later: "In truth, the harvest is abundant but the number of laborers is small, ask then the master of the harvest to
send laborers." What a mystery! ... Is not Jesus all-powerful?
Are not creatures His who made them? Why, then, does Jesus
say: "Ask the Lord of the harvest that he send some workers?"
Why? ... Ah! it is because Jesus has so incomprehensible a love
for us that He wills that we have a share with Him in the salvation of souls. He wills to do nothing without us. The Creator
of the universe awaits the prayer of a poor little soul to save
other souls redeemed like it at the price of all His Blood. Our
own vocation is not to go out to harvest the fields of ripe corn.
Jesus does not say to us: "*Lower* your eyes, look at the fields
and go harvest them." Our mission is still more sublime. These
are the words of our Jesus: "*Lift* your eyes and see." See how
in my heaven there are empty places; it is up to you to fill them,
you are my Moses praying on the mountain, ask me for workers and I shall send them, I await only a prayer, a sigh from
your heart! ...

Is not the apostolate of prayer, so to speak, more elevated
than that of the word? Our mission as Carmelites is to form
evangelical workers who will save thousands of souls whose
mothers we shall be. ... Céline, if these were not the very words
of our Jesus, who would dare to believe in them? ... I find that
our share is really beautiful, what have we to envy in priests?

...How I would like to be able to tell you all I am thinking, but time is lacking, understand all I could write you!...

> Your little Thérèse of the Child Jesus
> — LT #135

"MAKE HASTE TO DESCEND"

In another feast-day letter, Thérèse reflects again on the sisters' unity of soul and mind. Her ponderings on recent spiritual readings about the Blessed Virgin and the grandeur of the soul are also evident. Most significant, however, is the evident fruit of her recent private retreat, during which Thérèse had been quite taken by the insight that the Jesus of the gospels invites us to descend from the heights we have sought to climb in order to see him, and instead to take up the lowest place — where he will come to dwell with us. This was an important step in the development of her "little way."

October 19, 1892

Dear Céline,

Formerly, in the days of our childhood, we used to enjoy our feast because of the little gifts we mutually exchanged. The smallest object had then an incomparable value in our eyes.... Soon, the scene changed. Wings grew on the youngest of the birds, and it flew away far from the sweet nest of its childhood, and all illusions vanished! Summer had followed spring, life's reality, the dreams of youth....

Céline, was it not at that decisive moment that the bonds which joined our hearts were tightened? Yes, separation united us in a way that language cannot express. Our childlike affection was changed into a union of feelings, a unity of souls and minds. Who, then, could have accomplished this marvel?... Ah! it was He who had ravished our hearts. "The Beloved chosen among thousands, the odor alone of his ointments suffices to draw us after him. Following his steps, young maidens run lightly on the road" (Canticle of Canticles).

Jesus has attracted us together, although by different ways; together He has raised us above all the fragile things of this world whose image passes away. He has placed, so to speak, *all things* under our feet. Like Zacchaeus, we climbed a tree to see Jesus. . . . Then we could say with Saint John of the Cross: "All is mine, all is for me, the earth is mine, the heavens are mine, God is mine, and the Mother of God is mine." With regard to the Blessed Virgin, I must confide to you one of my simple ways with her. I surprise myself at times by saying to her: "But good Blessed Virgin, I find I am more blessed than you, for I have you for Mother, and you do not have a *Blessed Virgin to love*. . . . It is true you are the Mother of Jesus, but this Jesus you have given entirely to us . . . and He, on the Cross, He gave you to us as Mother. Thus we are richer than you since we possess Jesus and since you are ours also. Formerly, in your humility, you wanted one day to be the little servant of the happy Virgin who would have the honor of being the Mother of God, and here I am, a poor little creature, and I am not your servant but your child. You are the Mother of Jesus, and you are My Mother." No doubt, the Blessed Virgin must laugh at my simplicity, and nevertheless what I am telling her is really true! . . . Céline, what a mystery is our grandeur in Jesus. . . . This is all that Jesus has shown us in making us climb the symbolic tree about which I was just talking to you. And now what science is He about to teach us? Has He not taught us all? . . . Let us listen to what He is saying to us: "Make haste to descend, I must lodge today at your house." Well, Jesus tells us to descend. . . . Where, then, must we descend? Céline, you know it better than I, however, let me tell you where we must now follow Jesus. In days gone by, the Jews asked our divine Savior: "Master, where do you live." And He answered: "The foxes have their lairs, the birds of heaven their nests, but I have no place to rest my head." This is where we must descend in order that we may serve as an abode for Jesus. To be so poor that we do not have a place to rest our head. This is, dear Céline, what Jesus has done in my soul during my retreat.... You understand, there is question here of the interior. Besides, has not the exterior already been reduced to nothing by means of the very sad trial of Caen?...In our dear Father, Jesus has stricken us in the most sensitive exterior part of our heart; now let us allow him to act, He can complete His work in our souls....What Jesus desires is that we receive Him into our hearts. No doubt, they are already empty of creatures, but, alas, I feel mine is not entirely empty of myself, and it is for this reason that Jesus tells me to descend....He, the King of kings, humbled Himself in such a way that His face was hidden, and no one recognized Him...and I, too, want to hide my face, I want my Beloved alone to see it, that He be the only one to count my tears...that in my heart at least He may rest His dear head and feel that there He is known and understood....

Céline, I cannot tell you all I would like, my soul is powerless....Ah, if only I could!...But, no, this is not in my power ...why be sad, do you not always think what I am thinking? ...Thus all I do not tell you, you divine. Jesus makes you feel it in your heart. Has He not, moreover, set up His abode there to console Himself for the crimes of sinners? Yes, it is there in the intimate retreat of the soul that He instructs us together, and one day He will show us the day which will no longer have any setting....

Happy feast. How sweet it will be one day for your Thérèse to wish it to you in heaven!...   —LT #137

A DROP OF DEW

In February of 1893 Pauline, the first Martin sister to enter Carmel, was elected prioress. With her natural and spiritual "mothers" thus united, Thérèse flourished. It was around this time that the laudatory description quoted at the head of this chapter was written. In this long letter, written for Céline's twenty-fourth birthday, Thérèse plays with new creativity upon

her characteristic themes of flowers, littleness, hiddenness, night,
and thirst. Her continuing concern about possible threats to
Céline's vocation to Carmel is evident. The image of the dew,
symbolizing the soul's life totally absorbed and hidden in God,
also was featured in Thérèse's very first poem, which had been
written February 2, 1893, and was entitled "The Divine Dew, or
the Virginal Milk of Mary." The image may have been inspired
by a passage from John of the Cross's Spiritual Canticle.

April 25, 1893

Dear Céline,

I am going to tell you a thought that came to me this morning, or rather I am going to share with you the desires of Jesus
concerning your soul.... When I think of you in the presence of
the one friend of our souls, it is always simplicity that is presented to me as the distinctive characteristic of your heart....
Céline!... *simple* little *Céline*-flower, do not envy garden flowers. Jesus has not said to us: "I am the flower of the gardens,
the cultivated rose," but He tells us: "I am the *flower of the*
fields and the Lily of the valleys." Well, I thought this morning
near the Tabernacle that my Céline, the little flower of Jesus,
had to be and to remain always a *drop of dew* hidden in the divine corolla of the beautiful Lily of the valleys. A drop of dew,
what is more simple and more pure? It is not the *clouds* that
have formed it since, when the blue of the sky is star-studded,
the dew descends on the flowers; it is not comparable to the
rain that it surpasses in freshness and beauty. Dew exists only
at night; as soon as the sun darts its warm rays, it distills the
charming pearls that sparkle on the tips of blades of grass in the
meadow, and the dew is changed into a light vapor. Céline is a
little drop of dew that has not been formed by the clouds but
has descended from the beautiful heaven, its homeland. During *the night* of life, its mission is to hide itself in the heart of
the *Flower of the fields;* no human eye is to discover it there,
only the calyx possessing the little drop will know its freshness.
Blessed little drop of dew that is known only by Jesus!... Do

not stop to consider the course of resounding rivers that cause admiration in creatures. Do not even envy the clear brook winding in the meadow. No doubt its murmur is very sweet, but creatures can hear it . . . and then the calyx of the flower of the fields would be unable to contain it. It could not be for Jesus alone. To be His, one must remain little, little like a drop of dew! . . . Oh! how few are the souls who aspire to remain little in this way! . . . "But," they say, "are not the river and the brook more useful than the drop of dew, what does it do? It is good for nothing except to refresh for a few moments a flower of the fields which is today and will have disappeared tomorrow." Undoubtedly these persons are right, the drop of dew is good only for that; but they do not know the wild flower that willed to live on our earth of exile and to remain there during the short night of life. If they did know it, they would understand the reproach that Jesus made in days gone by to Martha. . . . Our Beloved has no need of our beautiful thoughts and our dazzling works. If He wants sublime thoughts, does He not have His angels, His legions of heavenly spirits whose knowledge infinitely surpasses that of the greatest geniuses of our sad earth? . . . It is not, then, intelligence and talents that Jesus has come to seek here below. He became the flower of the fields only in order to show us how much He cherishes simplicity. The Lily of the *valley* longs only for a little drop of dew. . . . And it is for this reason He has created one whose name is Céline! . . . During the night of life, she will have to remain hidden from every human glance, but when the shadows begin to lengthen, when the Flower of the fields becomes the Sun of Justice, and when He comes to carry out His giant's race, will He forget His little drop of dew? . . . Oh, no! as soon as He appears in glory, the companion of His exile will appear there too. The divine Sun will cast on her one of His rays of love, and immediately to the eyes of the dazzled angels and saints will be shown the poor little drop of dew that will sparkle like a precious diamond which, reflecting the Sun of Justice, will have become like Him. But this is not all. The divine Star, gazing at His drop of dew, will draw it to Himself; it will ascend like a light vapor and will go to place itself for eternity in the bosom of the burning furnace of uncreated love, and it will be forever united to Him. Just as on earth it had been the faithful companion of His exile, His insults, in the same way it will reign eternally in heaven....

Into what astonishment will be plunged those who, in this world, had considered the little drop of dew as useless!...No doubt, they will have an excuse: *the gift of God* had not been revealed to them; they had not brought their heart close to that of the *Flower of the fields,* and they had not understood those stirring words: "Give me to drink." Jesus does not call all souls to be drops of dew; He wills that there be precious liqueurs that creatures appreciate and that console them in their needs, but He keeps for Himself a drop of dew. This is His only desire....

What a privilege to be called to so lofty a mission!...But to respond to it, how *simple* we must remain....Jesus knows very well that on earth it is difficult to preserve oneself pure, so He wills that His drops of dew forget themselves. He is pleased to contemplate them, but He alone looks at them, and, as for themselves, not realizing their value, they deem themselves as beneath other creatures....That is what the Lily of the valleys desires. Has the little drop of dew, Céline, understood?...That is the purpose for which Jesus has created her, but she must not forget her little sister. She must obtain for her the favor of realizing what Jesus made her understand, so that one day the same Ray of love may distill the two drops of dew, and that together, after having been one on earth, they may be united for eternity in the bosom of the divine Sun.

Thérèse of the Child Jesus of the Holy Face
—LT #141

THE FIRE OF LOVE

A few days earlier, Céline had written that her soul was "plunged into death" and that "nothingness invades me more

*each day." Turning this nothingness around, Thérèse urges her
to offer the "nothings" of simple acts of charity to Jesus. When
he sees her throwing these little straws on the smoldering fire of
her heart, he will come to relight it.*

July 18, 1893

Dear Céline,

I was not counting on answering your letter this time, but our
Mother wants me to add a note to hers. What things I would
have to tell you! But since I have only a few moments, I must
first assure the little drop of dew that her Thérèse understands
her.... After having read your letter, I went to prayer, and taking the gospel, I asked Jesus to find a passage for you, and
this is what I found: "Behold the fig tree and the other trees,
when they begin to bear tender leaves, you judge that summer
is near. In the same way, when you will see these things taking place, know that the kingdom of God is near." I closed the
book, I had read enough; in fact, *these things* taking place in
my Céline's soul prove the kingdom of Jesus is set up in her
soul.... Now I want to tell you what is taking place in my own
soul; no doubt, it is the same thing as in yours. You have rightly
said, Céline, the cool mornings have passed for us, there remain
no more flowers to gather, Jesus has taken them for Himself.
Perhaps He will make new ones bloom one day, but in the
meantime what must we do? Céline, God is no longer asking
anything from me... in the beginning, He was asking an infinity of things from me. I thought, at times, that since Jesus was
no longer asking anything from me, I had to go along quietly
in peace and love, doing only what He was asking me.... But I
had a light. St. Teresa says we must maintain love. *The wood* is
not within our reach when we are in darkness, in aridities, but
at least are we not obliged to throw little pieces of straw on it?
Jesus is really powerful enough to keep the fire going by Himself. However, He is satisfied when He sees us put a little fuel on
it. This *attentiveness* pleases Jesus, and then He throws on the
fire a lot of wood. We do not see it, but we do feel the *strength*

of love's warmth. I have experienced it; when I *am feeling* nothing, when I am INCAPABLE *of praying,* of practicing virtue, then is the moment for seeking opportunities, *nothings,* which please Jesus more than mastery of the world or even martyrdom suffered with generosity. For example, a smile, a friendly word, when I would want to say nothing, or put on a look of annoyance, etc., etc.

Céline, do you understand? It is not for the purpose of weaving my crown, gaining merits, it is in order to please Jesus.... When I do not have any opportunities, I want at least to tell Him frequently that I love Him; this is not difficult, and it keeps the *fire* going. *Even though* this fire of love would seem to me to have gone out, I would like to throw something on it, and Jesus could then relight it. Céline, I am afraid I have not said what I should; perhaps you will think I always do what I am saying. Oh, no! I am not always faithful, but I never get discouraged; I abandon myself into the arms of Jesus. The little drop of dew goes deeper into the calyx of the flower of the fields, and there it finds again all it has lost and even much more.

Your little Sister Thérèse of the Child Jesus of the Holy Face
— LT #143

JESUS SLEEPS

Thérèse continues her counsel for the heavily burdened Céline, meditating especially on the gospel stories about Jesus sleeping in the disciples' boat (Matthew 8:20, 23–27; Mark 4:35–41).

July 23, 1893

Dear little Céline,

I am not surprised that you understand nothing that is taking place in your soul. A LITTLE *child all alone* on the sea, in a boat lost in the midst of the stormy waves, could she know whether she is close or far from port? While her eyes still contemplate the shore which she left, she knows how far she has gone, and, seeing the land getting farther away, she cannot contain her childish joy. Oh! she says, here I am soon at the end of my journey. But the more the shore recedes, the vaster the ocean also appears. Then the little child's KNOWLEDGE is reduced to nothing, she no longer knows where her boat is going. She does not know how to control the rudder, and the only thing she can do is abandon herself and allow her sail to flutter in the wind.... My Céline, *the little child* of Jesus, is all alone in a little boat; the *land* has disappeared from her eyes, she does not know where she is going, whether she is advancing or if she is going backward.... Little Thérèse knows, and she *is sure* her Céline is on the *open sea;* the boat carrying her is advancing with full sails toward the port, and the rudder which Céline cannot even see is not without a pilot. Jesus is there, *sleeping* as in the days gone by, in the boat of the fishermen of Galilee. He is sleeping... and Céline does not see Him, for night has fallen on the boat.... Céline *does not hear* the voice of Jesus. The wind is blowing... she *hears* it; she *sees* the darkness... and Jesus *is* always *sleeping*. However, if He were to awaken only for an instant, He would have only to command the wind and the sea, and there would be a great calm. The night would become brighter than the day, Céline *would see the divine glance* of Jesus, and her soul would be consoled.... But Jesus, too, would no longer be sleeping, and He is so FATIGUED!... His divine feet are tired from going after sinners, and in Céline's boat Jesus is sleeping so peacefully. The apostles had given Him a *pillow.* The Gospel gives us this detail. But in His dear *spouse's* little boat Our Lord finds another pillow much softer, Céline's *heart.* There He forgets all, He is at home.... It is not a stone which supports His divine head (that stone for which He longed during His mortal life), it is the heart of a *child,* the heart of a *spouse.* Oh, how happy Jesus is! But how can He be happy while His spouse is suffering, while she *watches* during the time He is sleeping so peacefully? Does He not know that Céline sees only the night, that His divine face remains hidden from her, and even at times the weight she feels on her heart seems heavy to her? . . . What a mystery! Jesus, the little child of Bethlehem whom Mary used to carry as a light burden, becomes heavy, so heavy that St. Christopher is astonished by it. . . . The spouse of the Canticles also says her Beloved is a bundle of myrrh and that He rests on her heart. Myrrh is *suffering,* and it is in this way that Jesus rests on Céline's heart. . . . And nevertheless Jesus is happy to see her in suffering. He is happy to receive all from her during the *night.* . . . He is awaiting the dawn and then, oh, then, what an awakening will be the awakening of Jesus!!! . . .

Be sure, dear Céline, that your boat is on the open sea, already perhaps very *close to port.* The wind of sorrow that pushes it is the *wind of love,* and this wind is swifter than lightning. . . .   —LT #144

THE HIDDEN TREASURE

In this letter we see Thérèse returning once again to a scripture text that had captivated her since she discovered it soon after she entered Carmel: Isaiah 53:3, translated in her time as "one whose face was hidden." This was a text upon which she had meditated deeply and frequently in relation to her father's humiliating illness. She weaves it together with other quotations and allusions from scripture, John of the Cross, and the Imitation of Christ, *all emphasizing the spiritual centrality of hiddenness and humility.*

August 2, 1893

Dear little Céline,

Your letter filled me with consolation. The road on which you are walking is a royal road, it is not a beaten track, but a *path* traced out by Jesus Himself. The spouse of the Canticles says that, not having found her Beloved in her bed, she arose to look for Him in the city but in vain; after having gone out of the city, she found Him whom her soul loved! . . . Jesus does not will that we find His adorable presence in repose; He hides

Himself; He wraps Himself in darkness. It was not thus that He acted with the *crowd* of Jews, for we see in the gospel that the people were CARRIED AWAY when He was speaking. Jesus used to charm weak souls with His divine words, He was trying to make them strong for the day of trial.... But how small was the number of Our Lord's friends when He was SILENT before his judges!... Oh! what a melody for my heart is this silence of Jesus.... He made Himself poor that we might be able to give Him love. He holds out His hand to us like a *beggar* so that on the radiant day of judgment when He will appear in His glory, He may have us hear those sweet words: "Come, blessed of my Father, for I was hungry and you gave me to eat; I was thirsty, and you gave me to drink; I did not know where to lodge, and you gave me a home. I was in prison, sick, and you helped me." It is Jesus Himself who spoke these words; it is He who wants our love, who *begs* for it.... He places Himself, so to speak, at our mercy, He does not want to take anything unless we give it to Him, and the smallest thing is precious in His divine eyes....

Dear Céline, let us take delight in our lot, it is so beautiful. Let us give, let us give to Jesus; let us be miserly with others but prodigal with Him....

Jesus is a *hidden* treasure, an inestimable good which few souls can find, for it is *hidden,* and the world loves what sparkles. Ah! if Jesus had willed to show Himself to all souls with His ineffable gifts, no doubt there is not one of them that would have despised Him. However, He does not will that we love Him for His gifts, *He Himself* must be our *reward*. To find a hidden thing one must hide oneself; our life must then be a *mystery*. We must be like Jesus, Jesus whose *face was hidden....* "Do you want to learn something that may be of use to you?" says the *Imitation*. "Love to be unknown and accounted for *nothing....* " And elsewhere: "After you have left everything, you must above all leave yourself; let one man boast of one thing, another of something else; as for you, place your joy only in contempt of yourself." What peace these words give to the soul, Céline. You know them, but do you not know all

I would like to say to you?... Jesus loves you with a love so great that, if you were to see it, you would be in an ecstasy of happiness that would cause your death, but you do not see it, and you are suffering.

Soon Jesus will stand up to save all the meek and humble of the earth!...   —LT #145

A BEAUTIFUL PEACH

Céline's household has recently been upset by the discovery that her maid is an alcoholic. Thérèse reminds Céline that, a few months earlier, the maid's husband had returned to the practice of the faith after Céline made a novena. In the parable of the peach and its "useless" beauty, Thérèse may be reflecting not only on Céline's situation but also on the comments of some sisters who, unaware of some of her responsibilities, felt that Thérèse was taking it easy in community.

August 13, 1893

Dear little Céline,

All the problems you are having with your maid have upset us.... Your poor maid is very unfortunate in having such a bad habit, especially in being deceitful, but could you perhaps convert her as you did her husband? For every sin, mercy, and God is powerful enough to give *stability* even to people who have none. I will really pray for her; perhaps were I in her place, I would be still less good than she is, and perhaps, too, she would have been already a great saint if she had received one half the graces God has granted to me.

I find that Jesus is very good in allowing my poor letters to do you some good, but, I assure you, I am not making the mistake of thinking I have anything to do with it. "If the Lord does not build the house, in vain do those work who build it." All the most beautiful discourses of the greatest saints would be incapable of making one *single* act of love come from a heart that Jesus did not possess. He alone can use His lyre, no one else can make its harmonious notes sound; however, Jesus uses all means, all creatures are at His service, and He loves to use them during the night of life in order to hide His adorable presence, but He does not hide Himself in such a way that He does not allow Himself to be divined. In fact, I really feel that often He gives me some lights, not for myself but for His little exiled dove, His dear spouse. This is really true. I find an example of it in nature itself. Here is a beautiful peach, pink and so sweet that all confectioners could not imagine a taste so sweet. Tell me, Céline, is it *for the peach* that God has created this pretty pink color, so velvety and so pleasing to see and to touch? Is it for the peach that He has given so much sugar? ... No, but for us and not for it. What belongs to it and what forms the *essence* of its life is its *stone;* we can take away all its beauty without taking from it *its being.* Thus Jesus is pleased to shower His gifts on some of His creatures, but very often this is in order to attract other hearts to Himself, and then when His end has been attained, He makes those external gifts disappear, He despoils completely the souls dearest to Him. When seeing themselves in so great poverty, these poor little souls are fearful, it seems to them that they are good for nothing, since they receive all from others and can give nothing. But it is not so: the *essence* of their *being* is working in secret. *Jesus* forms in them the seed which must be developed up above in the celestial gardens of heaven. He is pleased to show them their nothingness and His power. In order to reach them, He makes use of the *vilest* instruments so as to show them that He alone is working. He hastens to perfect His work for the day when the shadows having vanished, He will no longer use any intermediaries but an *eternal Face to Face!* ...

Sister Thérèse of the Child Jesus of the Holy Face
—LT #147

THE FRAGILE LYRE

By the spring of 1894 it was becoming evident that Louis Martin would not live much longer and that Céline would soon have to make a definite decision about her vocation. In honor of Céline's twenty-fifth birthday Thérèse wrote one of her most ambitious poems, "Saint Cecilia." While recognizing the goodness of holy matrimony, it saved its lyrical exaltation for consecrated virginity and martyrdom. The message intended for Céline was clear. Any wavering she may be enduring is only the weakness that will enable her to abandon herself totally into Jesus' hands as his instrument, with which he can make beautiful music.

April 26, 1894

Dear little Lyre of Jesus,

To sing your twenty-five years I am sending you a little poem that I composed when thinking of you!...

Céline! I am sure you will understand all my canticle would like to tell you, alas, I would need a tongue other than that of this earth to express the beauty of a soul's abandonment into the hands of Jesus. My heart was able only to babble what it feels.... *Céline, the story of Cecilia* (the *Saint* of ABANDON-MENT) is your story too! Jesus has placed near you an angel from heaven who is always looking after you; he carries you in his hands lest your foot strike against a stone. You do not see him, and yet he is the one who for twenty-five years has pre-served your soul, who has kept its virginal whiteness; he is the one who removes from you the occasions of sin.... He is the one who showed himself to you in a mysterious dream that he gave you in your childhood. You saw an angel carrying a torch and walking before our dear Father. Undoubtedly, he wanted to have you understand the mission that you would later carry out. You are now the visible angel of him who will soon go to be united to the angels of the heavenly city!... Céline, do not fear the storms of earth.... Your guardian angel is covering you with his wings, and Jesus, the purity of virgins, reposes in your heart. You do not see His treasures; Jesus is sleeping and the angel remains in his mysterious silence. However, they are there with Mary, who is hiding you also under her veil! ...

Do not fear, dear Céline, as long as *your lyre* does not cease to sing for Jesus, never *will it break*. ... No doubt it is fragile, more fragile than crystal. If you were to give it to an inexperienced musician, soon it would break; but Jesus is the one who makes the lyre of your heart sound. ... He is happy that you are feeling your weakness; *He* is the one placing in your soul sentiments of mistrust of itself. Dear Céline, thank Jesus. He *grants* you His choice *graces;* if always you remain faithful in pleasing Him in *little* things He will find Himself OBLIGED to help you in GREAT Things. ... The apostles worked all night without Our Lord and they caught no fish, but their work was pleasing to Jesus. He willed to prove to them that He alone can give us something; He willed that the apostles *humble themselves.* "Children," he said to them, "have you nothing to eat?" "Lord," St. Peter answered, "we have fished all night and *have caught nothing.*" Perhaps if he had caught some *little fish,* Jesus would not have performed the miracle, but he had *nothing,* so Jesus soon filled his net in such a way as almost to break it. This is the *character* of Jesus: He gives as God, but He wills *humility of heart.* ...

Before Him, the whole earth is like this *little grain of sand* which hardly gives the slightest motion in a scale or like *one* drop of the morning dew which falls upon the earth (Wisdom, chapter 11). ...

Thérèse of the Child Jesus
—LT #161

THE VAST FIELD OF THE SCRIPTURES

This letter, a sort of pastiche of Bible quotes and reflections, demonstrates the breadth and depth of Thérèse's meditations on scripture. The initial reference is to Léonie's unhappiness

in her life at the Visitation of Caen, which she had entered a
year earlier. The main focus continues to be spiritual counsel
for Céline's struggles with exhaustion, anxiety, and aridity.

July 7, 1894

Dear Céline,

Léonie's letter is disturbing us very much....

Ah! how unhappy she will be if she returns to the world! But
I admit that I hope this is only a temptation; we must pray very
much for her. God can very well give her what she is lacking....

I do not know if you are still in the same frame of mind as
the other day, but I will tell you just the same about a passage from the Canticle of Canticles which expresses perfectly
what a soul is when plunged into aridity and how nothing delights or consoles it. "I went down into the garden of nuts to
see the fruits of the valley, to look if the vineyard had flourished, and if the pomegranates had budded.... I no longer *knew*
where I *was*... my soul was all troubled because of the chariots
of Aminadab" (chap. 6, vv. 10 and 11).

This is really the image of our souls. Frequently, we descend
into the fertile valleys where our heart loves to nourish itself,
the vast field of the scriptures which has so many times opened
before us to pour out its rich treasures in our favor; this *vast
field* seems to us to be a desert, arid and without water.... We
know no longer where *we are;* instead of peace and light, we
find only turmoil or at least darkness.... But, like the spouse,
we know the cause of our trial: our soul is troubled because
of the chariots of Aminadab.... We are still not as yet in our
homeland, and *trial* must purify us as gold in the crucible. At
times, we believe ourselves abandoned. Alas! the chariots, the
vain noises that disturb us, are they within us or outside us?
We do not know... but Jesus really knows. He sees our sadness and suddenly His gentle voice makes itself heard, a voice
more gentle than the springtime breeze: "Return, return, my Su-
lamitess; return, return, that *we may look at you!* ..." (Cant.

chap. 6, v. 12). What a call is that of the Spouse!...And we were no longer daring even *to look at ourselves* so much did we consider ourselves without any splendor and adornment; and Jesus calls us, He wants to *look at* us at His leisure, but He is not alone; with Him, the two other Persons of the Blessed Trinity come to take possession of our soul....Jesus had promised it in days gone by when He was about to reascend to His Father and our Father. He said with ineffable tenderness: "If anyone *loves* me, he *will keep* my *word,* and my Father *will love* him, and *we* will come to him, and *we* will make in him *our* abode." To keep the *word* of Jesus, that is the sole condition of our happiness, the proof of our love for Him. But what, then, is this word?...It seems to me that the *word* of Jesus is *Himself....* He, *Jesus,* the *Word,* the *Word* of *God!* He tell us further on in the same gospel of St. John, praying to His Father for His disciples, He expresses Himself thus: "Sanctify them by your *word,* your word is *truth.*" In another place, Jesus teaches us that He is the way, the *truth,* the life. We know, then, what is the *Word* that we must keep; like Pilate, we shall not ask Jesus: "What is *Truth?*" We possess *Truth.* We *are keeping* Jesus in our *hearts!*...Often, like the spouse, we can say: "Our Beloved is a bundle of myrrh," that He is a Spouse of blood for us....But how sweet it will be to hear one day this very sweet word coming from the mouth of our Jesus: "You are the ones who have always remained with me in all the trials I have had, so I have prepared my kingdom for you, just as my Father has prepared it for me." The trials of Jesus, what a mystery! He has trials then, He too?...Yes, He has them, and often He is alone in treading the wine in the wine press; He looks for consolers and can find none....Many serve Jesus when He is consoling them, but *few* consent to keep company with *Jesus sleeping* on the waves or suffering in the garden of agony!...Who, then, will be willing to serve Jesus for Himself?...Ah! we shall be the ones....Céline and Thérèse will unite always more and more; in them, will be accomplished this prayer of Jesus: "Father, that they may be one as we are one." Yes, Jesus *is* already *preparing* His kingdom for us, just as His Father prepared it for him. He prepares it for us by leaving us in the *trial.* He wills that *our face be seen* by creatures, but that it be *as though hidden* so that no one *recognize* us but Himself alone!...But what joy, too, to think that *God,* the entire *Trinity,* is looking at us, that It is within us and is pleased to *look at* us. But what does *It* will to see in our heart if not "choirs of music in an army camp"? (Canticle, ch. 8, v. 1). "How, then, shall we be able to sing the Lord's canticles in a strange land?...For a long time, our harps were hung on the willows of the shore." We were not able to use them!...Our *God,* the *Guest* of our soul, knows it well, so He comes to us with the intention of finding an abode, an EMPTY *tent,* in the midst of the earth's field of battle. He asks only this, and He Himself is the Divine Musician who takes charge of the *concert.*...Ah! if only we were to hear this ineffable harmony, if one single vibration were to reach our ears!...

"We do not know how to ask for anything as we ought, but the Spirit pleads within us with unutterable groanings" (St. Paul). We have, then, only to surrender our soul, *to abandon* it to our great God. What does it matter, then, if our soul be without gifts that sparkle interiorly since within us the King of kings shines with all His glory! How great must a soul be to contain a God!...And yet the soul of a *day-old* child is a Paradise of delights for Him; what will it be, then, for our souls that have fought and suffered to delight the Heart of our Beloved?...

Dear Céline, I assure you, I do not know what I am saying to you, it must have no coherence, but it seems to me you will understand just the same!...I would like to tell you so many things!...

Thérèse of the Child Jesus of the Holy Face
—LT #165

This final selection serves well as a sort of a recapitulation of many of the images and themes woven throughout Thérèse's letters to Céline. Their rich correspondence would soon cease, for Louis Martin died on July 29 and Céline entered Lisieux Carmel on September 14, 1894. Mother Agnes then assigned Thérèse to direct Céline in the novitiate; the relationship of guidance and counsel continued, but now face to face.

3

Thérèse,
Warrior-Daughter
of St. Joan of Arc

Thérèse was born in 1873, less than two years after the humiliating defeat of France in the Franco-Prussian war. One of the chief ways in which France's wounded pride and sense of identity were being salved was by widespread promotion of the cult of Joan of Arc. While still a young teenager, the peasant girl Joan (1412–31) had heard saintly voices calling her to "save France" by leading the French armies to victory over the English and by bringing the dauphin Charles to Reims to be crowned king. The astonishing success of her initial military and political exploits is legendary. Subsequently, however, she was betrayed into the hands of the English, tried and convicted for heresy by an ecclesiastical court, and burned at the stake.

No doubt this story inspired many a late nineteenth-century French girl's youthful imagination with fantasies of glory. More unusual, however, was that from an early age Thérèse apparently was able to see past the superficial drama of the story to a more profound identification with Joan's sanctity. In particular, young Thérèse identified with Joan's childlike persona, her radical trust in the "hidden" God, and her fierce commitment to total self-giving on behalf of her people. Later in life, however, it was Joan's humiliation and martyrdom that Thérèse recognized as most central to their common calling.

Tracing Thérèse's identification with Joan of Arc is a fascinating enterprise in observing the confluence of culture, psychology, and grace in the spiritual journey. Thérèse participated in the fantasies, emotions, and prejudices of her era, yet at the same time milled and purified them in a far deeper current of urgency toward union with God.

BORN FOR GLORY

This passage from Story of a Soul *describes Thérèse's childhood encounter with the heroic story of Joan of Arc as a core formative moment in her psychospiritual development.*

When reading the accounts of the patriotic deeds of French heroines, especially the *Venerable* JOAN OF ARC, I had a great desire to imitate them; and it seemed I felt within me the same burning zeal with which they were animated, the same heavenly inspiration. Then I received a grace which I have always looked upon as one of the greatest in my life because at that age I wasn't receiving the *lights* I'm now receiving when I am flooded with them. I considered that I was born for *glory* and when I searched out the means of attaining it, God inspired in me the sentiments I have just described. He made me understand my own *glory* would not be evident to the eyes of mortals, that it would consist in becoming a great *saint!* This desire could certainly appear daring if one were to consider how weak and imperfect I was, and how, after seven years in the religious life, I still am weak and imperfect. I always feel, however, the same bold confidence of becoming a great saint because I don't count on my merits since I have *none,* but I trust in Him who is Virtue and Holiness. God alone, content with my weak efforts, will raise me to Himself and make me a *saint,* clothing me in His infinite merits. I didn't think then that one had to suffer

very much to reach sanctity, but God was not long in showing me this was so and in sending me the trials I have already
mentioned.

—SS 72

"THE MISSION OF JOAN OF ARC"

*January 21, 1894, was the first prioress's feast day celebrated
after Mother Agnes (Thérèse's blood sister Pauline) had been
elected. That very week, with much fanfare, Pope Leo XIII
declared Joan of Arc "Venerable" and began the official pro-
cess toward her canonization. In honor of these two special
events, Thérèse produced her very first play: "The Mission of
Joan of Arc." A year later, again for the prioress's feast, "Joan
of Arc Accomplishes Her Mission" was presented. Thérèse
herself played the title role in both plays. It has often been
noted that the plays — especially the first — are transparently
autobiographical.*

*This play consisted of fourteen Scenes and an Epilogue. The
first three Scenes present Joan as an innocent little shepherdess
who often hears sweet voices. Here her sister, Catherine, and
friend, Germaine, have just departed after urging Joan to hurry
along to a local festival.*

Scene 4: Joan Receives Her Call

JOAN: Already the hour is late and I have not yet heard my
voices...but nevertheless, I must leave for the festival. *(She
kneels down.)* O Blessed Lady! Protect me, I am your little
servant. Grant me the grace never to do anything that is not
pleasing to you.

SAINT MICHAEL, *unseen, sings:*

The day of victory is coming
Which will save the kingdom of the Franks!

But to God alone belongs all the glory,
To prove it He arms a mere child,
And this child, this young warrioress
Is not the descendant of a rich and valiant king —
She is nothing but a poor shepherdess.
But God calls her: All-powerful,
He wishes to give to a timid virgin
A heart of fire, the soul of a warrior;
Then he will crown her pure and ingenuous head
With lilies and laurels.

JOAN, *frightened:* O God! I do not understand!... Usually the voices I hear are so sweet.... But this one today is not addressed to me. Who then is the girl by whom such great things must be accomplished?... Perhaps it is me who is charged with acquainting her with the will of the good God.... But she will not believe me! O most holy Virgin Mary and you, my good guardian Angel, deign to enlighten me and tell me what I must do!...

SAINT CATHERINE AND SAINT MARGARET, *unseen, sing:*

Lovable child, our sweet companion
Your pure voice has mounted up to Heaven
And the guardian angel who always accompanies you
Has presented your requests to the Eternal One.

We come down from his Celestial empire
Where we reign for all eternity;
It is by our voices that God deigns to speak to you
　　　His will!...

It is necessary for you to go, to save your Fatherland,
And take up the sword to guard its honor;
The King of Heaven and the Virgin Mary
Will always know how to make your arms victorious.

JOAN, *more and more afraid:* Save the Fatherland!!!...Take up
the sword!...Me, a poor child of the fields....I am dream-
ing!... *(She stands up and glances about.)* No, I am very much
awake!...O, my God!...Come to my help!...I am troubled, I
am afraid!!!... *(She buries her face in her hands and weeps.)*

SAINT CATHERINE AND SAINT MARGARET, *unseen:*

Be consoled, Joan, and dry your tears!
Open your ears and look up to heaven,
There you will see that suffering has its charms;
You will rejoice in harmonious songs.

These melodies will fortify your soul
For the battle which soon must come.
You must have a love all in flames,
          You must suffer!...

For the pure soul, exiled on earth
The only glory is to carry the cross.
One day in heaven, this austere scepter
Will be more beautiful than the scepter of kings.

SAINT MICHAEL, *still unseen:*

Why are you speaking of tears and of suffering?
Sing rather of glorious battles,
Sing, sing the beauty of France
And the heroine adorned with victory!
Soon Joan will be conducted
By the God of battles, to new exploits;
All will see her traversing the fields of battle
          In the footsteps of the greatest generals.
Not for an instant does this magnanimous virgin
Seek the honors of the court!
Her heart remains pure, her faith great and sublime
          Until her last day.

Scene 13: Joan's Song of Self-giving

Scenes 5–10 consist mainly of interchange between young Joan and her "voices" — St. Michael, St. Catherine, and St. Margaret. In Scenes 11 and 12, the other children return and Joan confides her strange new calling to her sister, Catherine.

Catherine went away, weeping. After her departure, Joan knelt down and sang:

For you alone, O my God, I will leave my Father,
All my dear relatives and my beautiful parish church;
For you I will depart and fight in the war,
For you I will leave my little valley and my flock.
Instead of my sheep, I will lead an army;
I give you my joy and the springtime of my youth!
To please you, Lord, I will wield the sword
Instead of playing among the flowers of the fields.

My voice which loses itself amidst the whisper of the breeze
Soon must ring out at the heart of the battle;
Instead of the dreamy sound of a distant bell,
I will hear the great tumult of a people at war.
I desire the Cross!...I love sacrifice!...
Ah! deign to call me, I am ready to suffer —
Yes, to suffer for your love which appears delightful to me —
Jesus, my Beloved, for you I want to die.

Scene 14: Joan Invested for Her Mission by the Saints

Saint Michael appears with the other two saints. He carries a sword, while Saint Catherine carries a palm and Saint Margaret, a crown.

SAINT MICHAEL:

It is time, Joan; you must depart.
It is the Lord who arms you for war.

Daughter of God, do not be afraid to die;
The life for which you hope will come soon.

SAINT MARGARET: Dear child, you will reign.

SAINT CATHERINE: Following the Lamb with the whole troupe
of virgins.

THE TWO SAINTS, *together:*

Like us, you will sing
Of God's royal magnificence.

SAINT MICHAEL:

Joan, your name is written in the heavens
With the names of the saviors of France
And God keeps for you a glorious throne
Which will proclaim your grandeur and your power.

THE TWO SAINTS, *together:*

With happiness, we contemplate
The divine Glory which already radiates from your face
And which we bring you from Heaven —

SAINT CATHERINE: The palm of the martyr,

SAINT MARGARET: And the crown.

*The Saints advance to give Joan the palm and the crown, but
Saint Michael prevents them from approaching. He shows them
the sword and sings the following:*

SAINT MICHAEL:

It is necessary to fight before being a conqueror!
No, not yet the palm and the crown.

Arm yourself, Joan, great-hearted daughter;
Take this sword — it is God who gives it to you.

*Joan, on her knees, receives the sword. Then she rises, examines
it with happiness and love, and presses it to her heart.*

Epilogue: Saint Michael's Prophecy

*In this epilogue, Joan's ultimate triumph is linked to the
hope of Thérèse and the other Carmelites that the secular-
izing forces in French society will finally be cast out and a
tight bond between Church and state will be reinstituted.*

*After Joan's departure, Saint Michael looks up to Heaven and
sings in an inspired tone:*

SAINT MICHAEL:

I see already the Blessed of Heaven
Rejoicing as they listen to the lyre
Of Leo the Thirteenth, immortal pontiff
Who will sing of Joan, virgin and martyr.
      I hear the universe proclaiming
The virtues of the child who was humble and pious
      And I see God confirming
The good name of Blessed Joan!

For many long days, France will suffer
For she will be filled with the impious;
But glory will radiate from Joan,
And all pure souls will invoke the Saint;
      Voices will mount up to the Heavens
Singing in chorus with love and confidence.

THE THREE, *together:*

Joan of Arc, hear our cry:
A second time, save France! ...

                          —RP #1

"JOAN OF ARC ACCOMPLISHES
HER MISSION"

Part I of Thérèse's second play recounted Joan's encounter with the dauphin Charles, her military triumphs, his crowning as king, and finally Joan's prediction that she will be betrayed. Part II dramatically represents her suffering and death. Part III celebrates her triumphant reception in heaven and her crowning as patroness of France.

Thérèse's identification with Joan the martyr was already strong in early 1895 when she wrote this play, but events surrounding the play notched it up even higher. During the scene depicting Joan being burned at the stake, Thérèse's paper costume caught fire and, although she was not injured, she was greatly impressed by the potential of what could have happened. Then, in April of 1897, it was a photograph of Thérèse playing Joan in prison that Leo Taxil lifted up to ridicule before the whole world (see above p. 26).

Part II, Scene 1: Joan in Prison

The scene represents the prison. Joan is alone and in chains, sitting on a stone. On the ground are some straw, a jug, and some black bread.

JOAN, *singing:*

My voices predicted it, here I am a prisoner.
I do not expect any other help than Yours, O my God.
For your love alone, I left my aged Father,
My flowery countryside and my ever-blue sky.
For your love alone, I left my valley
and, lifting before the warriors the standard of the cross,
Lord, in your name, I commanded the army —
The highest generals listened to my voice!

An obscure prison, this is my recompense —
The prize of my labors, of my blood, of my tears.
I will never again see the places of my childhood,
My laughing meadow all enameled with flowers.
I will never see again the distant mountain
Whose snowy summit fades into the azure sky
Nor will I hear again the faint sound of the church bell,
Its sweet, dreamy sound undulating in the pure air.

In my dark prison, I search in vain for the star
That brightens the night in the beautiful firmament;
I search for the arbor that served as my veil
When I slept while guarding my flock.
Here, when I sleep in the midst of my tears,
I dream of perfumes, and the morning dew;
I dream of my valley, the woods full of charms —
But then the clatter of my chains awakens me with a start.

Scene 5: Joan, Image of the Crucified Christ

JOAN: Oh! How I am consoled to see that my agony resembles that of my Savior. . . . Although I do not feel his Divine presence, and death still makes me afraid!

THE ARCHANGEL:

The Redeemer dying on Calvary
Saw himself abandoned by the Eternal.
He cried out in his bitter sadness:
"My God, why have you abandoned me?"
You do not see the presence of Jesus,
His ravishing charms are hidden. . . .
Joan, your heart fears suffering,
You see death approaching, and you not yet twenty
    years old!

Daughter of God, during your life
You resembled your spouse Jesus,

And now he sees your agony;
All your groans are heard by him.
Great-hearted virgin, Jesus sees your anguish,
He sustains you with his all-powerful arm;
For you, soon, this passing life
Will be succeeded by an eternal present ! ! ! ...

Scene 11: Joan's Martyrdom

We hear THE VOICES which sing:

We descend from the eternal river
To smile on you and to carry you to the Heavens.
See in our hands the immortal crown
Which will glow on your glorious head. ...

Refrain

Come with us, dear Virgin,
O come! To our beautiful blue Heaven!
Leave your exile for the Homeland,
    Come delight in life,
        Daughter of God! ...

JOAN looks up to Heaven and says: I hear my voices, they invite
me to fly to the Heavens. ... No, my voices did not mislead me,
and my mission was from God! ... (The fire and smoke envelop
her more and more; at last she cries out:) Oh! The fire rises. ... I
burn! ... Water! holy water! ... Jesus, come to my aid ! ! ! ...

THE VOICES:

Flames have embraced this stake,
But more ardent is the love of your God.
For you, soon the eternal dawn
Will replace the torture of the fire.

Refrain

Finally, here is deliverance
Behold, the liberating angel.
Already the palm is waving
And Jesus advances toward you,
      Great-hearted daughter.

Virgin and martyr, a moment of suffering
Will conduct you to an eternal repose;
Daughter of God, your death saves France —
To her children you must open Heaven.

JOAN *sings this refrain:*

I enter into eternal life! ...
I see ... the angels, the elect....
I die to save my homeland
      Come! ... Virgin Mary....
      Jesus! ... Jesus ! ! ! ...

Joan bows her head and appears to collapse on the stake. Then she takes off her white robe and dresses in another robe all sprinkled with stars of gold.

Part III, Scene 1: Joan's Crowning in Heaven

When the screens are removed, we see a magnificent throne. Saint Catherine and Saint Margaret support Joan, and Saint Michael is also close to her. They sing:

SAINT MARGARET, *crowning Joan with roses:*

It is yours, it is yours,
The immortal crown, the immortal crown!

SAINT CATHERINE, *placing the palm in her hand:*

Martyr of the Lord, this palm is yours.

Saint Michael, *giving her a seat on the throne:*

> And the God of armies has prepared for you this throne,
>> It is yours.

The Saints, *together:*

> Oh! Rest in the Heavens, Joan, pure Dove
> Who has escaped forever the noose of the hunters.
> You will find here the brook that murmurs
>> The countryside, with the fields in flower.

>> *Refrain*

> Take your flight, take your flight!
> Open your white wings, open your white wings!
> And you will be able to fly to each star of gold....
> You will be able to visit the eternal vaults.
>> Take your flight, take your flight!

> Joan, no more enemies, no more dark prison;
> The brilliant Seraphim will call you their sister.
> Spouse of Jesus, your Beloved assures you
>> Eternal repose on his Heart!

Scene 2: Joan, Patroness of France

France *advances slowly, weighed down with chains and carrying her crown in her hands.*

> I come to you, all weighed down with chains,
> My face veiled, my eyes bathed in tears.
> I am no longer counted among the queens
> And my children overwhelm me with sorrows.
> They have forgotten God!...They abandon their
>> mother!...
> O Joan! Take pity on my bitter sadness
>> Come console my heart
>> Liberating angel —

I hope in you!
I hope in you!...

JOAN: Oh! My dear France! It is with happiness that I obey my voices which invite me to fly again to your aid!... From now on you will not be weighed down with chains because your heart is turned toward Heaven.... If you had invoked me sooner, I would have come to you long ago.

France, with hands chained, wants to place her diadem on Joan's head, but Joan, taking the crown, says to her:

No, I do not at all want to surround my head with the diadem of France... let me place it on your head, for in the future you will be worthy to wear it!...

Joan returns to her throne, after having embraced FRANCE; *then the latter unites her voice with the* VOICES *of her liberator to sing the following:*

Full of life, she has been raised to Heaven!
The holy voice of the successor of Peter
Has spoken, the immortal Pontiff....
The name of Joan is blazing with light!...

    Refrain

    Soon we will see raised to the altar
Joan, the new Patroness of France!...
    And the earth along with Heaven
  Will sing a hymn of gratitude.

                  — RP #3

THE FINAL BATTLE

At the end of her life Thérèse faced a battle of truly heroic proportions as she coped with excruciating physical pain, intense spiritual darkness, and — to top it all off — the humiliation of the "Diana Vaughan" affair (see above pp. 25–27). These texts, written during the last six months of her life, give us a glimpse of the matured fruit of Thérèse's imaginative identification with the fierce warrior-heroine Joan of Arc.

•

Thérèse composed the poem "My Weapons" for the profession of her cousin, Marie Guerin, on March 25, 1897. While it does not refer directly to Joan, it is a powerful expression of the heroic and military imagery in which Thérèse envisioned her Carmelite vocation.

"My Weapons"

"Put on the armor of God so that you may be able to stand firm against the tactics of the devil." (St. Paul)

"The Spouse of the King is terrible as an army ranged in battle, she is like a choir of music in an armed camp." (Song of Songs)

1   I have put on the weapons of the All-Powerful.
     His divine hand has deigned to adorn me.
     Henceforth nothing causes me alarm.
     Who can separate me from his love?
     At his side, rushing into the arena,
     I shall fear neither sword nor fire.
     My enemies will know that I am queen,
          That I am the spouse of a God!
     O my Jesus! I shall keep the armor
     That I put on under your adored eyes.
  Up to the evening of my life, my finest adornment
          Will be my sacred Vows!

2   O Poverty, my first sacrifice
     Even unto death, you will follow me everywhere.

For I know, to run into the arena
The Athlete must be detached from everything.
People of the world, taste remorse and sorrow,
Those bitter fruits of your vanity.
As for me, in the arena I joyously cut
    The palms of Poverty.
Jesus said: "It is by violence
That one takes the kingdom of Heaven."
So! Poverty will serve as my Lance,
    As my glorious Helmet.

3   Chastity makes me the sister of angels,
Of those pure, victorious Spirits.
One day I hope to fly in their armies,
But during this exile I must fight like them.
I must fight with no rest or truce
For my Spouse, the Lord of hosts,
Chastity is the celestial sword
    That can conquer hearts for him.
Chastity is my invincible armor.
My enemies are vanquished by it.
By it I become, O inexpressible joy!
    Jesus' Spouse!

4   The arrogant angel in the midst of light
Cried out: "I shall not obey!"
As for me, I cry out in the night of this life,
"Here below I always want to obey."
I sense springing up within me a holy audacity.
I face the fury of all hell.
Obedience is my strong Breastplate
    And the Shield of my heart.
Lord God of Hosts, I want no other glory
Than to submit my will in everything.
Since the Obedient One will tell of his victories
    For all Eternity.

5   If I have the powerful armor of the Warrior,
     If I imitate him and fight bravely,
     Like the Virgin of ravishing graces,
     I also want to sing as I fight.
     You make the strings of my lyre vibrate,
     And this lyre, O Jesus, is my heart!
     Then I can sing of the strength and sweetness
            Of your Mercies.
     Smiling, I bravely face the fire.
     And in your arms, O my Divine Spouse,
     I shall die singing on the battlefield,
         My weapons in hand! . . .

                                        — PN #48

                          •

More Glorious Conquests

This letter to Abbé Bellière, one of Thérèse's missionary "spiri-
tual brothers," was written about a month later and refers both
to the above poem and to her childhood epiphany in relation
to Joan. It shows how, just a few months before her death,
she is still returning to meditate on that formative moment. At
the time Thérèse wrote this letter, she had probably just learned
about how the charlatan Leo Taxil had held a photo of herself
playing Joan of Arc up for public ridicule. This may be part of
the dynamic behind the move from reflection on martyrdom to
remembering her identification with Joan.

                                        April 25, 1897

Dear little Brother,
    . . . You tell me, Brother, to beg for the favor of martyrdom
for you; this favor I have often sought for myself, but I am
not worthy of it, and truly we can say with St. Paul: "It is
not the work of him who wills or who runs, but of God who
shows mercy." Since the Lord seems to will to grant me only

the martyrdom of love, I hope He will permit me, by means of you, to gather the other palm we are striving after. I am pleased to see that God has given us the same attractions, the same desires. I made you smile, dear little Brother, when singing "My Weapons." Well! I shall make you smile once more when I tell you that I dreamt in my childhood of fighting on the fields of battle.... When I was beginning to learn the history of France, the account of Joan of Arc's exploits delighted me; I felt in my heart the desire and the courage to imitate her. It seemed the Lord destined me, too, for great things. I was not mistaken, but instead of voices from heaven inviting me to combat, I heard in the depths of my soul a gentler and stronger voice, that of the Spouse of Virgins, who was calling me to other exploits, to more glorious conquests, and into Carmel's solitude. I understood my mission was not to have a mortal king crowned but to make the King of heaven loved, to submit to Him the kingdom of hearts. —LT #224

•

This poem, composed in May of 1897, is Thérèse's final testament of her identification with Joan. Now it is the bitterness of having been betrayed into cruel suffering that predominates. Thérèse, like Joan, discovers the core of her call to sanctity as participation in the passion of Christ.

"To Joan of Arc"

When the Lord God of Hosts gave you the victory,
You drove out the foreigner and had the king crowned.
Joan, your name became renowned in history.
Our greatest conquerors paled before you.

But that was only a fleeting glory.
Your name needed a Saint's halo.
So the Beloved offered you his bitter cup,
And, like Him, you were spurned by men.

At the bottom of a black dungeon, laden with heavy
     chains,
The cruel foreigner filled you with grief.
Not one of your friends took part in your pain.
Not one came forward to wipe your tears.

Joan, in your dark prison you seem to me
More radiant, more beautiful than at your king's
     coronation.
This heavenly reflection of eternal glory,
Who then brought it upon you? It was betrayal.

Ah! If the God of love in this valley of tears
Had not come to seek betrayal and death,
Suffering would hold no attraction for us.
Now we love it, it is our treasure.

                                    —PN #50

4

Thérèse,
Martyr of Divine Mercy

When nine-year-old Thérèse dreamed of following in the foot-
steps of Joan of Arc, her attention was not yet captured by
the reality of Joan's bloody martyrdom. At fourteen, however,
when she visited the Colosseum and the Catacombs in Rome,
she found herself fervently praying that she might have the
grace of imitating the early saints by being a martyr for Jesus
(SS 130–31). She immediately felt that her prayer had been answered. From then on, the aspiration to martyrdom was central
in her spirituality. This chapter traces some of the stages in the
gradual maturation of that youthful dream.

A LETTER THÉRÈSE
CARRIED ON HER HEART
ON THE DAY OF HER PROFESSION

When Thérèse made her final vows as a Carmelite on September 8, 1890, she was only seventeen years old. On that day she
wrote this letter and placed it over her heart to spell out the
personal dimensions of her commitment.

O Jesus, my Divine Spouse! May I never lose the second robe of my baptism! Take me before I can commit the slightest voluntary fault. May I never seek nor find anything but Yourself alone. May creatures be nothing for me and may I be nothing for them, but may You, Jesus, be *everything!* May the things of earth never be able to trouble my soul, and may nothing disturb my peace. Jesus, I ask You for nothing but peace, and also love, infinite love without any limits other than Yourself; love which is no longer I but You, my Jesus. Jesus, may I die a martyr for You. Give me martyrdom of heart or of body, or rather give me both. Give me the grace to fulfill my Vows in all their perfection, and make me understand what a real spouse of Yours should be. Never let me be a burden to the community, let nobody be occupied with me, let me be looked upon as one to be trampled underfoot, forgotten like Your little grain of sand, Jesus. May Your will be done in me perfectly, and may I arrive at the place You have prepared for me.

Jesus, allow me to save very many souls; let no soul be lost today; let all the souls in purgatory be saved. Jesus, pardon me if I say anything I should not say. I want only to give You joy and to console You.   —SS Appendix, 275

ON FIRE WITH LOVE

Thérèse's "Act of Oblation to Merciful Love," written on June 9, 1895, and enacted two days later, is perhaps the most fully developed theological articulation of her personal spirituality. At the conclusion of Manuscript A of Story of a Soul, *she described for Mother Agnes what was going on in her mind and soul as she was inspired to make this Oblation.*

This year, June 9, the feast of the Holy Trinity, I received the grace to understand more than ever before how much Jesus desires to be loved.

I was thinking about the souls who offer themselves as victims of God's Justice in order to turn away the punishments reserved to sinners, drawing them upon themselves. This offering seemed great and very generous to me, but I was far from feeling attracted to making it. From the depths of my heart, I cried out:

"O my God! Will Your Justice alone find souls willing to immolate themselves as victims? Does not Your *Merciful Love* need them too? On every side this love is unknown, rejected; those hearts upon whom You would lavish it turn to creatures seeking happiness from them with their miserable affection; they do this instead of throwing themselves into Your arms and accepting Your infinite *Love*. O my God! Is Your disdained Love going to remain closed up within Your Heart? It seems to me that if You were to find souls offering themselves as victims of holocaust to Your Love, You would consume them rapidly; it seems to me, too, that You would be happy not to hold back the waves of infinite tenderness within You. If Your Justice loves to release itself, this Justice *which extends only over the earth,* how much more does Your Merciful Love desire to *set souls on fire* since Your Mercy *reaches to the heavens.* O my Jesus, let me be this happy victim; consume Your holocaust with the fire of Your Divine Love!"

You permitted me, dear Mother, to offer myself in this way to God, and you know the rivers or rather the oceans of graces which flooded my soul. Ah! since the happy day, it seems to me that *Love* penetrates and surrounds me, that at each moment this *Merciful Love* renews me, purifying my soul and leaving no trace of sin within it, and I need have no fear of purgatory. I know that of myself I would not merit even to enter that place of expiation since only holy souls can have entrance there, but I also know that the Fire of Love is more sanctifying than is the fire of purgatory. I know that Jesus cannot desire useless sufferings for us, and that He would not inspire the longings I feel unless He wanted to grant them.

Oh! how sweet is the way of Love! How I want to apply myself to doing the will of God always with the greatest self-surrender!   — SS 180–81

ACT OF OBLATION TO MERCIFUL LOVE

Thérèse's Act of Oblation is expressed in terms that many today may find strange or even offensive. The language of "victimhood" can conjure up images of unhealthy masochism or histrionic self-dramatization. In the context of her era, however, this was a common way of speaking about self-offering for the sake of the fulfillment of God's reign. Thérèse, profoundly uncomfortable with the way others spoke of a vengeful God whose "justice" would ask the innocent to suffer to make up for sin, gave the image a new twist. She affirmed that God's concern is not so much justice as love; what God asks of his friends is not that they suffer, but that they offer themselves totally in love. The one who gives herself in love will, indeed, be "martyred" as she is consumed by the waves of God's infinite tenderness; but Thérèse's vision is of ecstatic love, not of violent reprisal.

Offering of Myself as a Victim of Holocaust to God's Merciful Love

O My God! Most Blessed Trinity, I desire to *Love* You and make You *Loved,* to work for the glory of Holy Church by saving souls on earth and liberating those suffering in purgatory. I desire to accomplish Your will perfectly and to reach the degree of glory You have prepared for me in Your Kingdom. I desire, in a word, to be a saint, but I feel my helplessness and I beg You, O my God! to be Yourself my *Sanctity!*

Since You loved me so much as to give me Your only Son as my Savior and my Spouse, the infinite treasures of His merits are mine. I offer them to You with gladness, begging You to look upon me only in the Face of Jesus and in His heart burning with *Love.*

I offer You, too, all the merits of the saints (in heaven and on earth), their acts of *Love,* and those of the holy angels. Finally, I offer You, *O Blessed Trinity!* the *Love* and merits of the *Blessed Virgin, my dear Mother.* It is to her I abandon my offering, begging her to present it to You. Her Divine Son, my *Beloved* Spouse, told us in the days of His mortal life: *"Whatsoever you ask the Father in my name he will give it to you!"* I am certain, then, that You will grant my desires; I know, O my God! that *the more You want to give, the more You make us desire.* I feel in my heart immense desires and it is with confidence I ask You to come and take possession of my soul. Ah! I cannot receive Holy Communion as often as I desire, but, Lord, are You not *all-powerful?* Remain in me as in a tabernacle and never separate Yourself from Your little victim.

I want to console You for the ingratitude of the wicked, and I beg of You to take away my freedom to displease You. If through weakness I sometimes fall, may Your *Divine Glance* cleanse my soul immediately, consuming all my imperfections like the fire that transforms everything into itself.

I thank You, O my God! for all the graces You have granted me, especially the grace of making me pass through the crucible of suffering. It is with joy I shall contemplate You on the Last Day carrying the sceptre of Your Cross. Since You deigned to give me a share in this very precious Cross, I hope in heaven to resemble You and to see shining in my glorified body the sacred stigmata of Your Passion.

After earth's Exile, I hope to go and enjoy You in the Fatherland, but I do not want to lay up merits for heaven. I want to work for *Your Love* alone with the one purpose of pleasing You, consoling Your Sacred Heart, and saving souls who will love You eternally.

In the evening of this life, I shall appear before You with empty hands, for I do not ask You, Lord, to count my works.

All our justice is stained in Your eyes. I wish, then, to be clothed in Your own *Justice* and to receive from Your *Love* the eternal possession of *Yourself.* I want no other *Throne,* no other *Crown* but *You,* my *Beloved!*

Time is nothing in Your eyes, and a single day is like a thousand years. You can, then, in one instant prepare me to appear before You.

In order to live in one single act of perfect Love, I OFFER MYSELF AS A VICTIM OF HOLOCAUST TO YOUR MERCIFUL LOVE, asking You to consume me incessantly, allowing the waves of *infinite tenderness* shut up within You to overflow into my soul, and that thus I may become a *martyr* of Your *Love,* O my God!

May this martyrdom, after having prepared me to appear before You, finally cause me to die and may my soul take its flight without any delay into the eternal embrace of *Your Merciful Love.*

I want, O my *Beloved,* at each beat of my heart to renew this offering to You an infinite number of times, until the shadows having disappeared I may be able to tell You of my *Love* in an *Eternal Face to Face!*

Marie-Françoise-Thérèse of the Child Jesus
and the Holy Face, unworthy Carmelite religious

This 9th day of June,
Feast of the Most Holy Trinity,
In the year of grace, 1895.

—SS Appendix, 276–77

ENTRANCE TO THE NIGHT OF FAITH

During the last eighteen months of Thérèse's life, she learned a new meaning of martyrdom. During the night before Good Friday, 1896, her body began its precipitous decline through the effects of tuberculosis; only three days later, on Easter Sunday, she entered into total spiritual darkness. For the first time in her life she discovered her complete identity with those she regarded as sinners. Now when she prayed, "Have pity on us, O Lord, for we are poor sinners!" it was not from a position of superiority, but from a stance of solidarity and sisterhood.

Dear Mother, you know well that God has deigned to make me pass through many types of trials. I have suffered very much since I was on earth, but, if in my childhood I suffered with sadness, it is no longer in this way that I suffer. It is with joy and peace. I am truly happy to suffer. O Mother, you must know all the secrets of my soul in order not to smile when you read these lines, for is there a soul less tried than my own if one judges by appearances? Ah! if the trial I am suffering for a year now appeared to the eyes of anyone, what astonishment would be felt!

Dear Mother, you know about this trial; I am going to speak to you about it, however, for I consider it as a great grace I received during your office as Prioress.

God granted me, last year, the consolation of observing the fast during Lent in all its rigor. Never had I felt so strong, and this strength remained with me until Easter. On Good Friday, however, Jesus wished to give me the hope of going to see Him soon in heaven. Oh! how sweet this memory really is! After remaining at the Tomb until midnight, I returned to our cell, but I had scarcely laid my head upon the pillow when I felt something like a bubbling stream mounting to my lips. I didn't know what it was, but I thought that perhaps I was going to die and my soul was flooded with joy. However, as our lamp was extinguished, I told myself I would have to wait until the morning to be certain of my good fortune, for it seemed to me that it was blood I had coughed up. The morning was not long in coming; upon awakening, I thought immediately of the joyful thing that I had to learn, and so I went over to the window. I was able to see that I was not mistaken. Ah! my soul was filled with a great consolation; I was interiorly persuaded that Jesus, on the anniversary of His own death, wanted to have me hear His first call. *It was like a sweet and distant murmur which announced the Bridegroom's arrival.*

It was with great fervor that I assisted at Prime and the Chapter of Pardons. I was in a rush to see my turn come in order to be able, when asking pardon from you, to confide my hope and my happiness to you, dear Mother; however, I added that I was not suffering in the least (which was true) and I begged you, Mother, to give me nothing special. In fact, I had the consolation of spending Good Friday just as I desired. Never did Carmel's austerities appear so delightful to me; the hope of going to heaven soon transported me with joy. When the evening of that blessed day arrived, I had to go to my rest; but just as on the preceding night, good Jesus gave me the same sign that my entrance into eternal life was not far off.

At this time I was enjoying such a living faith, such a clear *faith,* that the thought of heaven made up all my happiness, and I was unable to believe there were really impious people who had no faith. I believed they were actually speaking against their own inner convictions when they denied the existence of heaven, that beautiful heaven where God Himself wanted to be their Eternal Reward. During those very joyful days of the Easter season, Jesus made me feel that there were really souls who have no faith, and who, through the abuse of grace, lost this precious treasure, the source of the only real and pure joys. He permitted my soul to be invaded by the thickest darkness, and that the thought of heaven, up until then so sweet to me, be no longer anything but the cause of struggle and torment. This trial was to last not a few days or a few weeks, it was not to be extinguished until the hour set by God Himself and this hour has not yet come. I would like to be able to express what I feel, but alas! I believe this is impossible. One would have to travel through this dark tunnel to understand its darkness. I will try to explain it by a comparison.

I imagine I was born in a country which is covered in thick fog. I never had the experience of contemplating the joyful appearance of nature flooded and transformed by the brilliance of the sun. It is true that from childhood I have heard people speak of these marvels, and I know the country in which I am living is not really my true fatherland, and there is another I must long for without ceasing. This is not simply a story invented by someone living in the sad country where I am, but it is a reality, for the King of the Fatherland of the bright sun actually came and lived for thirty-three years in the land of darkness. Alas! the darkness did not understand that this Divine King was the Light of the world.

Your child, however, O Lord, has understood Your divine light, and she begs pardon for her brothers. She is resigned to eat the bread of sorrow as long as You desire it; she does not wish to rise up from this table filled with bitterness at which poor sinners are eating until the day set by You. Can she not say in her name and in the name of her brothers, *"Have pity on us, O Lord, for we are poor sinners!"* Oh! Lord, send us away justified. May all those who were not enlightened by the bright flame of faith one day see it shine. O Jesus! if it is needful that the table soiled by them be purified by a soul who loves You, then I desire to eat this bread of trial at this table until it pleases You to bring me into Your bright Kingdom. The only grace I ask of You is that I never offend You! —SS 210–12

SELECTIONS FROM
THE LAST CONVERSATIONS

Beginning in April 1897, Thérèse was so ill that she could write very little. Her sisters, convinced of the great value of her insights, began to keep records of their conversations with her. There has been considerable debate over the authenticity of these "Last Conversations"; some believe that they reflect the spirituality of the other nuns of Carmel more than that of Thérèse. Nevertheless, they provide for us a glimpse of Thérèse during her last days of intense suffering.

"I always see the good side of things. There are some who set about giving themselves the most trouble. For me, it's just the opposite. If I have nothing but pure suffering, if the heavens are so black that I see no break in the clouds, well, I make this my joy! I revel in it! I did this during Papa's trial which made me more glorious than a queen."   May 27, 1897 — LC #51

(She was asked to explain what happened when she made her Act of Oblation to Merciful Love....)

"Well, I was beginning the Way of the Cross; suddenly, I was seized with such a violent love for God that I can't explain it except by saying it felt as though I were totally plunged into fire. Oh! What fire and what sweetness at one and the same time! I was on fire with love, and I felt that one minute more, one second more, and I wouldn't be able to sustain this ardor without dying. I understood, then, what the saints were saying about these states which they experienced so often. As for me, I experienced it only once and for one single instant, falling back immediately into my habitual state of dryness."

(And later on): "At the age of fourteen, I also experienced transports of love. Ah! how I loved God! But it wasn't at all as it was after my Oblation to Love; it wasn't a real flame that was burning me."   July 7, 1897 — LC #77

"One could believe that it is because I haven't sinned that I have such great confidence in God. Really tell them, Mother, that if I had committed all possible crimes, I would always have the same confidence; I feel that this whole multitude of offenses would be like a drop of water thrown into a fiery furnace. You will then tell the story about the converted sinner who died of love; souls will understand immediately, for it's such a striking example of what I'm trying to say. However, these things cannot be expressed in words."   July 11, 1897 — LC #89

"If I had been rich, I would have found it impossible to see a poor person going hungry without giving him my possessions.

And in the same way, when I gain any spiritual treasures, feeling that at this very moment there are souls in danger of being lost and falling into hell, I give them what I possess, and I have not yet found a moment when I can say: Now I'm going to work for myself."   July 14, 1897 — LC #96

(At 2:00 in the morning, she coughed up blood): "I feel that I'm about to enter into my rest. But I feel especially that my mission is about to begin, my mission of making God loved as I love Him, of giving my little way to souls. If God answers my desires, my heaven will be spent on earth until the end of the world. Yes, I want to spend my heaven in doing good on earth. This isn't impossible, since from the bosom of the beatific vision, the angels watch over us.

"I can't make heaven a feast of rejoicing; I can't rest as long as there are souls to be saved. But when the angel will have said: 'Time is no more!' (Apoc. 10:6) then I will take my rest; I'll be able to rejoice, because the number of the elect will be complete and because all will have entered into joy and repose. My heart beats with joy at this thought."   July 17, 1897 — LC #102

"These words of Isaiah: 'Who has believed our report? . . . There is no beauty in him, no comeliness, etc.' (Isa. 53:1–2) have made the whole foundation of my devotion to the Holy Face, or, to express it better, the foundation of all my piety. I, too, have desired to be without beauty, alone in treading the winepress, unknown to everyone."   August 5 — LC #161–62

"AN UNPETALLED ROSE"

This poem was written May 19, 1897, as Thérèse's tubercular illness was entering its final phases. She was, literally, being stripped of everything. The image of the "unpetalled rose" expresses her complete acceptance of her lot, and thus its transformation into an act of love for her God.

1 Jesus, when I see you held by your Mother,
        Leaving her arms
   Trying, trembling, *your first steps*
        On our sad earth,
   Before you I'd like *to unpetal a rose*
        In its freshness
   So that your little foot might rest ever so softly
        On a flower! . . .

2 *This unpetalled rose* is a faithful image,
        Divine Child,
   Of the heart that wants to sacrifice itself for you
            unreservedly
        At each moment.
   Lord, on your altars more than one new rose
        Likes to shine.
   It gives itself to you . . . but I dream of something else:
        To be unpetalled! . . .

3 The rose in its splendor can adorn your feast,
        Lovable Child,
   But *the unpetalled rose* is just flung out
        To blow away.
   An unpetalled rose gives itself unaffectedly
        To be no more.
   Like it, with joy I abandon myself to you,
        Little Jesus.

4 One walks *on rose petals* with no regrets,
        And this debris
   Is a simple ornament that one disposes of artlessly,
        That I've understood.
   Jesus, for your love I've squandered my life,
        My future.
   In the eyes of men, a rose forever *withered*,
        I must *die!* . . .

5 *For you,* I must *die,* Child, Beauty Supreme,
         What a blessed fate!
   In *being unpetalled,* I want to prove to you that I love you,
         O my Treasure! ...
   Under your *baby steps,* I want to live here below
         With mystery,
   And I'd like to soften once more on Calvary
         Your last steps! ...

                                        —PN #51

Thérèse,
Love in the Heart
of the Church

The centrality of love is so obvious a gospel theme that it can easily seem trite. Yet even to begin to understand and live love is the work of a lifetime. Whenever any person discovers love, it is a fresh and unique moment, and a burst of joy and transforming power is released into the world. Throughout her life, Thérèse passionately sought the way of love and discovered it in ever-new dimensions. In this chapter we glimpse the intense energy and creativity of that quest as she strove to express it in poetry and narrative.

THE SCIENCE OF LOVE

In this letter to Sister Marie of the Sacred Heart (Thérèse's blood sister Marie), Thérèse introduces the astonishing fruits of her September 1896 retreat. Here she names her one and only ambition as to learn "the science of love" and affirms that Jesus, too, thirsts only for our love. For her, all this is closely linked to her developing "little way."

Do not believe I am swimming in consolations; oh, no! my consolation is to have none on earth. Without showing Himself, without making His voice heard, Jesus teaches me in secret. It is not by means of books, for I do not understand what I am reading, but at times a word like this one that I drew out at the end of prayer (after having remained in silence and aridity) comes to console me: "Here is the Master I am giving you; he will teach you all you must do. I want to have you read in the book of life wherein is contained the science of Love." The science of Love, oh! yes, this word resounds sweetly in the ear of my soul. I desire only this science. Having given all my riches for it, I look upon this as having given nothing, just as the spouse in the sacred canticles...I understand so well that it is only love that can make us pleasing to God that this love is the only good that I ambition. Jesus is pleased to show me the only road which leads to this divine furnace, and this road is the *abandonment* of the little child who sleeps without fear in his Father's arms.... "Whoever is a *little one,* let him come to me" said the Holy Spirit through the mouth of Solomon, and this same Spirit of Love has said again: "Mercy is granted to little ones." In His name, the Prophet Isaiah reveals to us that on the last day: "The Lord will lead his flock into pastures, he will gather together the *little lambs* and will press them to his bosom," and as though all these promises were not enough, the same Prophet, whose inspired glance was already plunged into the eternal depths, cried out in the Lord's name: "As a mother caresses her child, so will I comfort you; I will carry you on my bosom, and I shall rock you on my knees."

Oh, dear Godmother, after language like this, there is nothing to do but be silent and weep with gratitude and love.... Ah! if all weak and imperfect souls felt what the littlest of all souls feels, the soul of your little Thérèse, not one would despair of reaching the summit of the mountain of love, since Jesus does not ask for great actions but only abandonment and gratitude,

since He has said in Psalm 49: "I have no need of the he-goats
from your flocks, for all the beasts of the forest belong to me,
and the thousands of animals that graze on the hills; I know all
the birds of the mountains.... If I were hungry, I would not tell
you, for the earth and all it contains are mine. Must I eat the
flesh of bulls and drink the blood of goats?"...

"*Offer to God sacrifices of praise and thanksgiving.*" See,
then, all that Jesus is asking from us. He has no need of our
works but only of our *love,* for this same God, who declares
He has no need to tell us if He is hungry, did not hesitate
to *beg* for a little water from the Samaritan woman. He was
thirsty.... But when He said: "Give me to drink," it was the
love of His poor creatures that the Creator of the universe
was asking. He was thirsty for love.... Ah! I feel it more than
ever, Jesus is *parched;* He meets with only the ungrateful and
indifferent among His disciples of the world and among His
own disciples He finds, alas! few hearts that give themselves
to Him without any reservations, that understand all the tenderness of His infinite Love. Dear Sister, how blessed we are
to understand the intimate secrets of our Spouse. Ah! if you
were willing to write all that you know about them, we would
have beautiful pages to read, but I know that you prefer to
keep in the bottom of your heart "the secrets of the King."
You say to me: "It is honorable to publish the works of the
Most High." I find you are right in keeping silence, and it is
only in order to please you that I write these lines, for I feel
my powerlessness in repeating in earthly words the secrets of
heaven. And, then, after having written out pages and pages,
I would find that I had still not begun.... There are so many
different horizons, so many infinitely varied nuances, that the
palette of the heavenly Painter alone will be able, after the night
of this life, to furnish me with colors capable of painting the
marvels that He reveals to the eyes of my soul.

—LT #196; cf. also SS 187–89

"MY HEAVEN ON EARTH!..."

This poem, written on August 12, 1895, plays upon the image of the "Holy Face" which was so moving for Thérèse. To be face to face with Jesus in perfect intimacy, to share a mutual gaze of tender love — this was her human longing and her spiritual dream. Yet, like all lovers, Thérèse had to come to terms with the frequent apparent absence of the loved one, as well as the shattering reality of his immersion in suffering. This poem, subtitled "Canticle to the Holy Face," unifies all these themes in a song of passionate and singlehearted love.

1 Jesus, your ineffable image
　Is that star that guides my steps.
　Ah! You know, your sweet Face
　Is for me Heaven on earth.
　My love discovers the charms
　Of your Face adorned with tears.
　I smile through my own tears
　When I contemplate your sorrows....

2 Oh! To console you I want
　To live unknown on earth!...
　Your beauty, which you know how to veil,
　Discloses for me all its mystery.
　I would like to fly away to you!...

3 Your Face is my only Homeland.
　It's my Kingdom of love.
　It's my cheerful Meadow,
　Each day, my sweet Sun.
　It's the Lily of the Valley
　Whose mysterious perfume
　Consoles my exiled soul,
　Making it taste the peace of Heaven.

4 It's my Rest, my Sweetness
　And my melodious Lyre....

Your Face, O my sweet Savior,
Is the Divine bouquet of Myrrh
I want to keep on my heart! ...

5 Your Face is my only wealth.
I ask for nothing More.
Hiding myself in it unceasingly,
I will resemble you, Jesus. ...
Leave in me the Divine impress
Of your Features filled with sweetness,
And soon I'll become holy.
I shall draw hearts to you.

6 So that I may gather
A beautiful golden harvest,
Deign to set me aflame with your fire.
With your adored Mouth,
Give me soon the eternal Kiss! ...

—PN #20

THE JOY OF CHARITY

*The fullness of gospel love includes not only the dimension of
spiritual eros that seeks the "eternal Kiss" of the divine Lover,
but also that of charity which loves those who are least attractive and who have little to give in return. Thérèse discovered
"charity" in her Christmas conversion at age thirteen, and this
grace continued to mature throughout her life. In this passage
from* Manuscript C of Story of a Soul, *written in the last months
of her life, she offers her counsel in this regard.*

I have noticed (and this is very natural) that the most saintly Sisters are the most loved. We seek their company; we render them
services without their asking; finally, these souls so capable of
bearing with the lack of respect and consideration of others see
themselves surrounded with everyone's affection. We may apply

to them these words of our Father St. John of the Cross: "All goods were given to me when I no longer sought them through self-love."

On the other hand, imperfect souls are not sought out. No doubt we remain within the limits of religious politeness in their regard, but we generally avoid them, fearing lest we say something which isn't too amiable. When I speak of imperfect souls, I don't want to speak of spiritual imperfections since the most holy souls will be perfect only in heaven; but I want to speak of a lack of judgment, good manners, touchiness in certain characters; all these things which don't make life very agreeable. I know very well that these moral infirmities are chronic, that there is no hope of a cure, but I also know that my Mother would not cease to take care of me, to try to console me, if I remained sick all my life. This is the conclusion I draw from this: I must seek out in recreation, on free days, the company of Sisters who are the least agreeable to me in order to carry out with regard to these wounded souls the office of the good Samaritan. A word, an amiable smile, often suffice to make a sad soul bloom; but it is not principally to attain this end that I wish to practice charity, for I know I would soon become discouraged: a word I shall say with the best intention will perhaps be interpreted wrongly. Also, not to waste my time, I want to be friendly with everybody (and especially with the least amiable Sisters) to give joy to Jesus and respond to the counsel He gives in the Gospel in almost these words:

"When you give a dinner or a supper do not invite your friends, or your brethren, or your relatives, or your rich neighbors, lest perhaps they also invite you in return, and a recompense be made to you. But when you give a feast, invite the poor, the crippled, the lame, the blind; and blessed shall you be, because they have nothing to repay you with, and your Father who sees in secret will reward you." What banquet could a Carmelite offer her Sisters except a spiritual banquet of loving and joyful charity? As far as I am concerned, I know no other and I want to imitate St. Paul who *rejoiced with those*

who rejoice; it is true he wept with the afflicted and tears must
sometimes appear in the feast I wish to serve, but I shall always
try *to change these tears into joy,* since the Lord *loves a cheerful
giver.*   —SS 245–47

LOVE FOR THE LEAST OF THESE

*This story, also from Manuscript C, reveals Thérèse's practice
of charity in its most concrete form.*

I remember an act of charity God inspired me to perform while
I was still a novice. It was only a very small thing, but *our
Father who sees in secret* and who looks more upon the intention than upon the greatness of the act *has already* rewarded
me without my having to wait for the next life. It was at the
time Sister St. Pierre was still going to the choir and the refectory. She was placed in front of me during evening prayer. At
ten minutes to six a Sister had to get up and lead her to the
refectory, for the infirmarians had too many patients and were
unable to attend to her. It cost me very much to offer myself for
this little service because I knew it was not easy to please Sister St. Pierre. She was suffering very much and she did not like
it when her helpers were changed. However, I did not want to
lose such a beautiful opportunity for exercising charity, remembering the words of Jesus: *"Whatever you do to the least of my
brothers, you do to me."* I offered myself very humbly to lead
her, and it was with a great deal of trouble that I succeeded in
having my services accepted! I finally set to work and had so
much good will that I succeeded perfectly.

Each evening when I saw Sister St. Pierre shake her hour-
glass I knew this meant: Let's go! It is incredible how difficult
it was for me to get up, especially at the beginning; however, I
did it immediately, and then a ritual was set in motion. I had
to remove and carry her little bench in a certain way, above
all I was not to hurry, and then the walk took place. It was a

question of following the poor invalid by holding her cincture; I did this with as much gentleness as possible. But if by mistake she took a false step, immediately it appeared to her that I was holding her incorrectly and that she was about to fall. "Ah! my God! You are going too fast; I'm going to break something." If I tried to go more slowly: "Well, come on! I don't feel your hand; you've let me go and I'm going to fall! Ah! I was right when I said you were too young to help me."

Finally, we reached the refectory without mishap; and here other difficulties arose. I had to seat Sister St. Pierre and I had to act skillfully in order not to hurt her; then I had to turn back her sleeves (again in a certain way), and afterwards I was free to leave. With her poor crippled hands she was trying to manage with her bread as well as she could. I soon noticed this, and, each evening, I did not leave her until after I had rendered her this little service. As she had not asked for this, she was very much touched by my attention, and it was by this means that I gained her entire good graces, and this especially (I learned this later) because, after cutting her bread for her, I gave her my most beautiful smile before leaving her all alone.

Dear Mother, perhaps you are surprised that I write about this little act of charity, performed so long ago. Ah! if I have done so, it is because I feel I must sing of the Lord's mercies because of it. He deigned to leave its memory with me as a perfume which helps me in the practice of charity. I recall at times certain details which are like a springtime breeze for my soul. Here is one which comes to my memory: One winter night I was carrying out my little duty as usual; it was cold, it was night. Suddenly, I heard off in the distance the harmonious sound of a musical instrument. I then pictured a well-lighted drawing room, brilliantly gilded, filled with elegantly dressed young ladies conversing together and conferring upon each other all sorts of compliments and other worldly remarks. Then my glance fell upon the poor invalid whom I was supporting. Instead of the beautiful strains of music I heard only her occasional complaints, and instead of the rich gildings I saw only the bricks of our austere cloister, hardly visible in the faintly glimmering light. I cannot express in words what happened in my soul; what I know is that the Lord illumined it with rays of *truth* which so surpassed the dark brilliance of earthly feasts that I could not believe my happiness. Ah! I would not have exchanged the ten minutes employed in carrying out my humble office of charity to enjoy a thousand years of worldly feasts. If already in suffering and in combat one can enjoy a moment of happiness that surpasses all the joys of this earth, and this when simply considering that God has withdrawn us from this world, what will this happiness be in heaven when one shall see in the midst of eternal joy and everlasting repose the incomparable grace the Lord gave us when He chose us to dwell in His house, heaven's real portal?   — SS 247–49

A VISION OF LOVE

During her retreat of September 1896 — five months after entering her night of faith — Thérèse was granted a momentary respite as she was gifted with this vision of the love of the communion of saints. (This text is part of a letter she wrote to her sister Marie, which is now known as Manuscript B of Story of a Soul.*)*

O Jesus, my Beloved, who could express the tenderness and sweetness with which You are guiding my soul! It pleases You to cause the rays of Your grace to shine through even in the midst of the darkest storm! Jesus, the storm was raging very strongly in my soul ever since the beautiful feast of Your victory, the radiant feast of Easter; one Saturday in the month of May, thinking of the mysterious dreams which are granted at times to certain souls, I said of myself that these dreams must be a very sweet consolation, and yet I wasn't asking for such a consolation. In the evening, considering the clouds which were covering her heaven, my little soul said again within herself that these beautiful dreams were not for her. And then she fell asleep in the midst of the storm. The next day was May 10, the second SUNDAY of Mary's month, and perhaps the anniversary of the day when the Blessed Virgin deigned to smile upon her little flower.

At the first glimmerings of dawn I was (in a dream) in a kind of gallery and there were several other persons, but they were at a distance. Our Mother was alone near me. Suddenly without seeing how they had entered, I saw three Carmelites dressed in their mantles and long veils. It appeared to me they were coming for our Mother, but what I did understand clearly was that they came from heaven. In the depths of my heart I cried out: "Oh! how happy I would be if I could see the face of one of these Carmelites!" Then, as though my prayer were heard by her, the tallest of the saints advanced towards me; immediately I fell to my knees. Oh! what happiness! the Carmelite *raised her veil or rather she raised it and covered me with it*. Without the least hesitation, I recognized *Venerable Anne of Jesus,* Foundress of Carmel in France. Her face was beautiful but with an immaterial beauty. No ray escaped from it and still, in spite of the veil which covered us both, I saw this heavenly face suffused with an unspeakably gentle light, a light it didn't receive from without but was produced from within.

I cannot express the joy of my soul since these things are experienced but cannot be put into words. Several months have passed since this sweet dream, and yet the memory it has left in my soul has lost nothing of its freshness and heavenly charms. I still see Venerable Mother's glance and smile which was FILLED WITH LOVE. I believe I can still feel the caresses she gave me at this time.

Seeing myself so tenderly loved, I dared to pronounce these words: "O Mother! I beg you, tell me whether God will leave me for a long time on earth. Will He come soon to get me?" Smiling tenderly, the saint whispered: *"Yes, soon, soon, I promise you."* I added: "Mother, tell me further if God is not asking something more of me than my poor little actions and desires.

Is He content with me?" The saint's face took on an expression *incomparably more tender* than the first time she spoke to me. Her look and her caresses were the sweetest of answers. However, she said to me: "God asks no other thing from you. He is content, very content!" After again embracing me with more love than the tenderest of mothers has ever given to her child, I saw her leave. My heart was filled with joy, and then I remembered my Sisters, and I wanted to ask her some favors for them, but alas, I awoke!

O Jesus, the storm was no longer raging, heaven was calm and serene. I *believed*, I *felt* there was a *heaven* and that this *heaven* is peopled with souls who actually love me, who consider me their child. This impression remains in my heart, and this all the more because I was, up until then, *absolutely indifferent to Venerable Mother Anne of Jesus.* I never invoked her in prayer and the thought of her never came to my mind except when I heard others speak of her which was seldom. And when I understood to what a degree *she loved me,* how *indifferent* I had been towards her, my heart was filled with love and gratitude, not only for the Saint who had visited me but for all the blessed inhabitants of heaven.   — SS 190–92

"MY VOCATION IS LOVE"

This continuation of Manuscript B contains perhaps the most powerful and lyrical of all Thérèse's writings. It is here that she shares the painful intensity of her manifold desires and the moment of ecstasy when she discovered them all unified in the single vocation of "love in the heart of the Church." In this moment her insight into the vocation to martyrdom is also significantly reconfigured.

O my Beloved! this grace was only the prelude to the greatest graces You wished to bestow upon me. Allow me, my only Love, to recall them to You today, *today* which is the sixth anniversary of our union. Ah! my Jesus, pardon me if I am unreasonable in wishing to express my desires and longings which reach even unto infinity. Pardon me and heal my soul by giving her what she longs for so much!

To be Your *Spouse*, to be a *Carmelite*, and by my union with You to be the *Mother* of souls, should not this suffice me? And yet it is not so. No doubt, these three privileges sum up my true *vocation: Carmelite, Spouse, Mother*, and yet I feel within me other *vocations*. I feel the *vocation* of the WARRIOR, THE PRIEST, THE APOSTLE, THE DOCTOR, THE MARTYR. Finally, I feel the need and the desire of carrying out the most heroic deeds for *You, O Jesus*. I feel within my soul the courage of the *Crusader*, the *Papal Guard*, and I would want to die on the field of battle in defense of the Church.

I feel in me the *vocation of* the PRIEST. With what love, O Jesus, I would carry You in my hands when, at my voice, You would come down from heaven. And with what love would I give You to souls! But alas! while desiring to be a *Priest*, I admire and envy the humility of St. Francis of Assisi and I feel the *vocation* of imitating him in refusing the sublime dignity of the *Priesthood*.

O Jesus, my Love, my Life, how can I combine these contrasts? How can I realize the desires of my poor *little soul?*

Ah! in spite of my littleness, I would like to enlighten souls as did the *Prophets* and the *Doctors*. I have the *vocation of the Apostle*. I would like to travel over the whole earth to preach Your Name and to plant Your glorious Cross on infidel soil. But *O my Beloved*, one mission alone would not be sufficient for me, I would want to preach the Gospel on all the five continents simultaneously and even to the most remote isles. I would be a missionary, not for a few years only but from the beginning of creation until the consummation of the ages. But above all, O my Beloved Savior, I would shed my blood for You even to the very last drop.

Martyrdom was the dream of my youth and this dream has grown with me within Carmel's cloisters. But here again, I feel that my dream is a folly, for I cannot confine myself to desiring one kind of martyrdom. To satisfy me I need *all*. Like You, my Adorable Spouse, I would be scourged and crucified. I would die flayed like St. Bartholomew. I would be plunged into boiling oil like St. John; I would undergo all the tortures inflicted upon the martyrs. With St. Agnes and St. Cecelia, I would present my neck to the sword, and like Joan of Arc, my dear sister, I would whisper at the stake Your Name, O JESUS. When thinking of the torments which will be the lot of Christians at the time of Anti-Christ, I feel my heart leap with joy and I would that these torments be reserved for me. Jesus, Jesus, if I wanted to write all my desires, I would have to borrow Your *Book of Life,* for in it are reported all the actions of all the saints, and I would accomplish all of them for You.

O my Jesus! what is your answer to all my follies? Is there a soul more *little,* more powerless than mine? Nevertheless even because of my weakness, it has pleased You, O Lord, to grant my *little childish desires* and You desire, today, to grant other desires that are *greater* than the universe.

During my meditation, my desires caused me a veritable martyrdom, and I opened the Epistles of St. Paul to find some kind of answer. Chapters 12 and 13 of the First Epistle to the Corinthians fell under my eyes. I read there, in the first of these chapters, that *all* cannot be apostles, prophets, doctors, etc., that the Church is composed of different members, and that the eye cannot be the hand at *one and the same time.* The answer was clear, but it did not fulfill my desires and gave me no peace. But just as Mary Magdalene found what she was seeking by always stooping down and looking into the empty tomb, so I, abasing myself to the very depths of my nothingness, raised myself so high that I was able to attain my end. Without becoming discouraged, I continued my reading, and this sentence consoled me: *"Yet strive after THE BETTER GIFTS, and I point out to you a yet more excellent way."* And the Apostle explains how all *the most PERFECT gifts* are nothing without *LOVE.*

That Charity is the EXCELLENT WAY that leads most surely to God.

I finally had rest. Considering the mystical body of the Church, I had not recognized myself in any of the members described by St. Paul, or rather I desired to see myself in them *all. Charity* gave me the key to my *vocation.* I understood that if the Church had a body composed of different members, the most necessary and most noble of all could not be lacking to it, and so I understood that the Church *had a Heart and that this Heart was BURNING WITH LOVE. I understood it was Love alone* that made the Church's members act, that if *Love* ever became extinct, apostles would not preach the Gospel and martyrs would not shed their blood. I understood that LOVE COMPRISED ALL VOCATIONS, THAT LOVE WAS EVERYTHING, THAT IT EMBRACED ALL TIMES AND PLACES.... IN A WORD, THAT IT WAS ETERNAL!

Then, in the excess of my delirious joy, I cried out: O Jesus, my Love...my *vocation,* at last I have found it.... MY VOCATION IS LOVE!

Yes, I have found my place in the Church and it is You, O my God, who have given me this place; in the heart of the Church, my Mother, I shall be *Love.* Thus I shall be everything, and thus my dream will be realized.

Why speak of a delirious joy? No, this expression is not exact, for it was rather the calm and serene peace of the navigator perceiving the beacon which must lead him to the port. ...O luminous Beacon of love, I know how to reach You, I have found the secret of possessing Your flame.

I am only a child, powerless and weak, and yet it is my weakness that gives me the boldness of offering myself as *VICTIM of Your Love, O Jesus!* In times past, victims, pure and spotless, were the only ones accepted by the Strong and Powerful God. To satisfy Divine *Justice,* perfect victims were necessary, but the *law of Love* has succeeded to the law of fear, and *Love* has chosen me as a holocaust, me, a weak and imperfect creature. Is not

this choice worthy of *Love?* Yes, in order that Love be fully satisfied, it is necessary that It lower Itself, and that It lower Itself
to nothingness and transform this nothingness into *fire.*

O Jesus, I know it, love is repaid by love alone, and so I
searched and I found the way to solace my heart by giving you
Love for Love. "Make use of the riches which render one unjust
in order to make friends who will receive you into everlasting
dwellings." Behold, Lord, the counsel You give Your disciples
after having told them that "The children of this world, in relation to their own generation, are more prudent than are the
children of the light." A child of light, I understood that *my desires of being everything,* of embracing all vocations, were the
riches that would be able to render me unjust, so I made use
of them to make friends. Remembering the prayer of Elisha to
his Father Elias when he dared to ask him for HIS DOUBLE
SPIRIT, I presented myself before the angels and saints and I
said to them: "I am the smallest of creatures; I know my misery and my feebleness, but I know also how much noble and
generous hearts love to do good. I beg you then, O Blessed
Inhabitants of heaven, I beg you to ADOPT ME AS YOUR
CHILD. *To you alone will be the glory* which you will make me
merit, but deign to answer my prayer. It is bold, I know; however, I dare to ask you to obtain for me YOUR TWOFOLD
SPIRIT."

Jesus, I cannot fathom the depths of my request; I would
be afraid to find myself overwhelmed under the weight of my
bold desires. My excuse is that I am a *child,* and children do
not reflect on the meaning of their words; however, their parents, once they are placed upon a throne and possess immense
treasures, do not hesitate to satisfy the desires of the *little ones*
whom they love as much as they love themselves. To please
them they do foolish things, even going to the extent of *becoming weak* for them. Well, I am the *Child of the Church* and the
Church is a Queen since she is Your Spouse, O divine King of
kings. The heart of a child does not seek riches and glory (even
the glory of heaven). She understands that this glory belongs by

right to her brothers, the angels and saints. Her own glory will be the reflected glory which shines on her Mother's forehead. What this child asks for is Love. She knows only one thing: to love You, O Jesus. Astounding works are forbidden to her; she cannot preach the Gospel, shed her blood; *but what does it matter since her brothers work in her stead and she*, a little child, stays very close to the *throne* of the King and Queen. She loves in her brothers' place while they do the fighting. But how will she prove her *love* since *love* is proved by works? Well, the little child *will strew flowers*, she will perfume the royal throne with their *sweet scents*, and she will sing in her silvery tones the canticle of *Love*.

Yes, my Beloved, this is how my life will be consumed. I have no other means of proving my love for you other than that of strewing flowers, that is, not allowing one little sacrifice to escape, not one look, one word, profiting by all the smallest things and doing them through love. I desire to suffer for love and even to rejoice through love; and in this way I shall strew flowers before Your throne. I shall not come upon one without *unpetalling* it for You. While I am strewing my flowers, I shall sing, for could one cry while doing such a joyous action? I shall sing even when I must gather my flowers in the midst of thorns, and my song will be all the more melodious in proportion to the length and sharpness of the thorns.

O Jesus, of what use will my flowers be to You? Ah! I know very well that this fragrant shower, these fragile, worthless petals, these songs of love from the littlest of hearts will charm You. Yes, these nothings will please You. They will bring a smile to the Church Triumphant. She will gather up my flowers unpetalled through love and have them pass through Your own divine hands, O Jesus. And this Church in heaven, desirous of playing with her little child, will cast these flowers, which are now infinitely valuable because of Your divine touch, upon the Church Suffering in order to extinguish its flames and upon the Church Militant in order to gain the victory for it!

O my Jesus! I love You! I love the Church, my Mother! I recall that *"the smallest act of PURE LOVE is of more value to her than all other works together."* But is PURE LOVE in my heart? Are my measureless desires only but a dream, a folly? Ah! if this be so, Jesus, then enlighten me, for You know I am seeking only the truth. If my desires are rash, then make them disappear, for these desires are the greatest martyrdom to me. However, I feel, O Jesus, that after having aspired to the most lofty heights of Love, if one day I am not to attain them, I feel that I shall have tasted *more sweetness in my martyrdom and my folly* than I shall taste in the bosom of the *joy of the Fatherland,* unless You take away the memory of these earthly hopes through a miracle. Allow me, then, during my exile, the delights of love. Allow me to taste the sweet bitterness of my martyrdom.

Jesus, O Jesus, if the *desire of loving You* is so delightful, what will it be to possess and enjoy this Love?

—SS 192–97

"LIVING ON LOVE"

Many regard this poem, composed in February of 1895, as Thérèse's best.

1 On the evening of Love, speaking without parable,
   Jesus said: "If anyone wishes to love me
   All his life, let him keep my Word.
   My Father and I will come to visit him.
   And we will make his heart our dwelling.
   Coming to him, we shall love him always.
   We want him to remain, filled with peace,
         In our Love!... "

2 Living on love is holding You Yourself.
   Uncreated Word, Word of my God,
   Ah! Divine Jesus, you know I love you.

The Spirit of Love sets me aflame with his fire.
In loving you I attract the Father.
My weak heart holds him forever.
O Trinity! You are Prisoner
    Of my Love!...

3 Living on Love is living on your life,
Glorious King, delight of the elect.
You live for me, hidden in a host.
I want to hide myself for you, O Jesus!
Lovers must have solitude,
A heart-to-heart lasting night and day.
Just one glance of yours makes my beatitude.
    I live on Love!...

4 Living on Love is not setting up one's tent
At the top of Tabor.
It's climbing Calvary with Jesus,
It's looking at the Cross as a treasure!
In Heaven I'm to live on joy.
Then trials will have fled forever.
But in exile, in suffering I want
    To live on Love.

5 Living on Love is giving without limit
Without claiming any wages here below.
Ah! I give without counting, truly sure
That when one loves, one does not keep count!...
Overflowing with tenderness, I have given everything,
To the Divine Heart...lightly I run.
I have nothing left but my only wealth:
    Living on Love.

6 Living on Love is banishing every fear,
Every memory of past faults.
I see no imprint of my sins.
In a moment love has burned everything....
Divine Flame, O very sweet Blaze!

I make my home in your hearth.
In your fire I gladly sing:
>   "I live on Love!..."

7 Living on Love is keeping within oneself
A great treasure in an earthen vase.
My Beloved, my weakness is extreme.
Ah, I'm far from being an angel from heaven!...
But if I fall with each passing hour,
You come to my aid, lifting me up.
At each moment you give me your grace:
>   I live on love.

8 Living on Love is sailing unceasingly,
Sowing peace and joy in every heart.
Beloved Pilot, Charity impels me,
For I see you in my sister souls.
Charity is my only star.
In its brightness I sail straight ahead.
I've my motto written on my sail:
>   "Living on Love."

9 Living on Love, when Jesus is sleeping,
Is rest on stormy seas.
Oh! Lord, don't fear that I'll wake you.
I'm waiting in peace for Heaven's shore....
Faith will soon tear its veil.
My hope is to see you one day.
Charity swells and pushes my sail:
>   I live on Love!...

10 Living on Love, O my Divine Master,
Is begging you to spread your Fire
In the holy, sacred soul of your Priest.
May he be purer than a seraphim in Heaven!...
Ah! glorify your Immortal Church!
Jesus, do not be deaf to my sighs.

I, her child, sacrifice myself for her.
>> I live on Love.

11 Living on Love is wiping your Face,
It's obtaining the pardon of sinners.
O God of Love! may they return to your grace,
And may they forever bless your Name....
Even in my heart the blasphemy resounds.
To efface it, I always want to sing:
"I adore and love your Sacred Name.
>> I live on Love!..."

12 Living on Love is imitating Mary,
Bathing your divine feet that she kisses, transported.
With tears, with precious perfume,
She dries them with her long hair....
Then standing up, she shatters the vase,
And in turn she anoints your Sweet Face.
As for me, the perfume with which I anoint your Face
>> Is my Love!...

13 "Living on Love, what strange folly!"
The world says to me, "Ah! stop your singing,
Don't waste your perfumes, your life.
Learn to use them well...."
Loving you, Jesus, is such a fruitful loss!...
All my perfumes are yours forever.
I want to sing on leaving this world:
>> "I'm dying of Love!"

14 Dying of Love is truly sweet martyrdom,
And that is the one I wish to suffer.
O Cherubim! Tune your lyre,
For I sense my exile is about to end!...
Flame of Love, consume me unceasingly.
Life of an instant, your burden is so heavy to me!
Divine Jesus, make my dream come true:
>> To die of Love!...

15 Dying of Love is what I hope for,
    When I shall see my bonds broken,
    My God will be my Great Reward.
    I don't desire to possess other goods.
    I want to be on fire with his Love.
    I want to see Him, to unite myself to Him forever.
    That is my Heaven...that is my destiny:
            Living on Love!!!...
                                        —PN #17

6

Thérèse,
Teacher of the Little Way

*The cult of littleness and spiritual childhood was hardly origi-
nal with Thérèse. It had been part of French spirituality since at
least the seventeenth century, and in the late nineteenth century
it was being widely promoted in Thérèse's milieu. From an early
age, Thérèse and her sisters constantly used (indeed, overused)
the word "little." Yet, as with other cultural commonplaces,
there came a point in Thérèse's spiritual journey where she saw
into the depths of what others took for granted, and something
radically new emerged.*

*It was in late 1894 that Thérèse discovered the texts from
Proverbs and Isaiah that she quotes in the first passage in
this chapter, and they catalyzed for her what she came to call
her "little way." In essence, the little way is simply total trust
in God. Regardless of one's weaknesses, imperfections, sins,
or failures, complete trust will gain all things from God. The
charm of the little way is that it is not available just to great
souls, but to everyone. In fact, the more ordinary and imperfect
one is, the more one is an ideal candidate for the little way and
its astonishing spiritual effectiveness!*

CARE OF SOULS

In February of 1893 when Mother Agnes (Thérèse's blood sister Pauline) was elected prioress, twenty-year-old Thérèse was assigned to work with the novices as a spiritual formator. Taking her charge very seriously, she began to learn the art of teaching. It was in the context of this challenging task, in fact, that the doctrine of the "little way" first began to emerge with full clarity for her.

I told you, dear Mother, that I had learned very much when I was teaching others. I saw first of all that all souls have very much the same struggles to fight, but they differ so much from each other in other aspects that I have no trouble in understanding what Father Pichon was saying: *"There are really more differences among souls than there are among faces."* It is impossible to act with all in the same manner. With certain souls, I feel I must make myself little, not fearing to humble myself by admitting my own struggles and defects; seeing I have the same weaknesses as they, my little Sisters in their turn admit their faults and rejoice because I understand them *through experience.* With others, on the contrary, I have seen that to do them any good I must be very firm and never go back on a decision once it is made. To abase oneself would not then be humility but weakness. God has given me the grace not to fear the battle; I must do my duty at all costs. I have heard the following on more than one occasion: "If you want to get anything out of me, you will have to win me with sweetness; force will get you nothing." I myself know that nobody is a good judge in his own case, and that a child, whom a doctor wants to perform a painful operation upon, will not fail to utter loud cries and to say that the remedy is worse than the sickness; however, when he is cured a few days later, he is very happy at being able to play and run. It is exactly the same for souls; soon they recognize that a little bit of bitterness is at times preferable to sugar and they don't fear to admit it.   — SS 239–40

THE ELEVATOR

Elevators were new inventions then, and when Thérèse heard about them in May of 1897 she was captivated. Indeed, the image of the "elevator of grace" capsulizes Thérèse's little way perfectly.

You know, Mother, I have always wanted to be a saint. Alas! I have always noticed that when I compared myself to the saints, there is between them and me the same difference that exists between a mountain whose summit is lost in the clouds and the obscure grain of sand trampled underfoot by the passers-by. Instead of becoming discouraged, I said to myself: God cannot inspire unrealizable desires. I can, then, in spite of my littleness, aspire to holiness. It is impossible for me to grow up, and so I must bear with myself such as I am with all my imperfections. But I want to seek out a means of going to heaven by a little way, a way that is very straight, very short, and totally new.

We are living now in an age of inventions, and we no longer have to take the trouble of climbing stairs, for, in the homes of the rich, an elevator has replaced these very successfully. I wanted to find an elevator which would raise me to Jesus, for I am too small to climb the rough stairway of perfection. I searched, then, in the Scriptures for some sign of this elevator, the object of my desires, and I read these words coming from the mouth of Eternal Wisdom: *"Whoever is a LITTLE ONE, let him come to me"* [Proverbs 9:4]. And so I succeeded. I felt I had found what I was looking for. But wanting to know, O my God, what You would do to *the very little one* who answered Your call, I continued my search and this is what I discovered: *"As one whom a mother caresses, so will I comfort you; you shall be carried at the breasts, and upon the knees they shall caress you"* [Isaiah 66:13, 12]. Ah! never did words more tender and more melodious come to give joy to my soul. The elevator which must raise me to heaven is Your arms, O Jesus! And for

this I had no need to grow up, but rather I had to remain *little*
and become this more and more.   —SS 207–8

THE LITTLE BIRD

*The story of the little bird is Thérèse's most fully developed
explanation of her little way. In the original text, this follows
immediately after her discovery of her vocation as "love in the
heart of the Church."*

How can a soul as imperfect as mine aspire to the possession of
the plenitude of *Love?* O Jesus, *my first and only Friend,* You
whom I love UNIQUELY, explain this mystery to me! Why do
You not reserve these great aspirations for great souls, for the
Eagles that soar in the heights?

I look upon myself as a *weak little bird,* with only a light
down as covering. I am not an *eagle,* but I have only an eagle's
EYES AND HEART. In spite of my extreme littleness I still dare
to gaze upon the Divine Sun, the Sun of Love, and my heart
feels within it all the aspirations of an *Eagle.*

The little bird wills to fly towards the bright Sun which attracts its eye, imitating its brothers, the eagles, whom it sees
climbing up towards the Divine Furnace of the Holy Trinity.
But alas! the only thing it can do is *raise its little wings;* to fly
is not within its *little* power!

What then will become of it? Will it die of sorrow at seeing
itself so weak? Oh no! the little bird will not even be troubled.
With bold surrender, it wishes to remain gazing upon its Divine
Sun. Nothing will frighten it, neither wind nor rain, and if dark
clouds come and hide the Star of Love, the little bird will not
change its place because it knows that beyond the clouds its
bright Sun still shines on and that its brightness is not eclipsed
for a single instant.

At times the little bird's heart is assailed by the storm, and it
seems it should believe in the existence of no other thing except

the clouds surrounding it; this is the moment of *perfect joy* for the *poor little weak creature*. And what joy it experiences when remaining there just the same! and gazing at the Invisible Light which remains hidden from its faith!

O Jesus, up until the present moment I can understand Your love for the little bird because it has not strayed far from You. But I know and so do You that very often the imperfect little creature, while remaining in its place (that is, under the Sun's rays), allows itself to be somewhat distracted from its sole occupation. It picks up a piece of grain on the right or on the left; it chases after a little worm; then coming upon a little pool of water, it wets its feathers still hardly formed. It sees an attractive flower and its little mind is occupied with this flower. In a word, being unable to soar like the eagles, the poor little bird is taken up with the trifles of earth.

And yet after all these misdeeds, instead of going and hiding away in a corner, to weep over its misery and to die of sorrow, the little bird turns towards its beloved Sun, presenting its wet wings to its beneficent rays. It cries like a swallow and in its sweet song it recounts in detail all its infidelities, thinking in the boldness of its full trust that it will acquire in even greater fullness the love of *Him* who came to call not the just but sinners. And even if the Adorable Star remains deaf to the plaintive chirping of the little creature, even if it remains hidden, well, the little one will remain *wet,* accepting its numbness from the cold and rejoicing in its suffering which it knows it deserves.

O Jesus, Your *little bird* is happy to be *weak and little.* What would become of it if it were big? Never would it have the boldness to appear in Your presence, *to fall asleep* in front of You. Yes, this is still one of the weaknesses of the little bird: when it wants to fix its gaze upon the Divine Sun, and when the clouds prevent it from seeing a single ray of that Sun, in spite of itself, its little eyes close, its little head is hidden beneath its wing, and the poor little thing falls asleep, believing all the time that it is fixing its gaze upon its Dear Star. When it awakens, it doesn't feel desolate; its little heart is at peace and it begins once again its work of *love*. It calls upon the angels and saints who rise like eagles before the consuming Fire, and since this is the object of the little bird's desire the eagles take pity on it, protecting and defending it, and putting to flight at the same time the vultures who want to devour it. These vultures are the demons whom the little bird doesn't fear, for it is not destined to be their *prey* but the prey of the *Eagle* whom it contemplates in the center of the Sun of Love.

O Divine Word! You are the Adored Eagle whom I love and who alone *attracts me!* Coming into this land of exile, You willed to suffer and to die in order *to draw* souls to the bosom of the Eternal Fire of the Blessed Trinity. Ascending once again to the Inaccessible Light, henceforth Your abode, You remain still in this "valley of tears," hidden beneath the appearances of a white host. Eternal Eagle, You desire to nourish me with Your divine substance and yet I am but a poor little thing who would return to nothingness if Your divine glance did not give me life from one moment to the next.

O Jesus, allow me in my boundless gratitude to say to You that Your *love reaches unto folly.* In the presence of this folly, how can You not desire that my heart leap towards You? How can my confidence, then, have any limits? Ah! the saints have committed their *follies* for You, and they have done great things because they are eagles.

Jesus, I am too little to perform great actions, and my own *folly* is this: to trust that Your Love will accept me as a victim. My *folly* consists in begging the eagles, my brothers, to obtain for me the favor of flying towards the Sun of Love with the *Divine Eagle's own wings!*

As long as You desire it, O my Beloved, Your little bird will remain without strength and without wings and will always stay with its gaze fixed upon You. It wants to be *fascinated* by Your divine glance. It wants to become the *prey* of Your Love.

One day I hope that You, the Adorable Eagle, will come to fetch me, Your little bird; and ascending with it to the Furnace of Love, You will plunge it for all eternity into the burning Abyss of this Love to which it has offered itself as victim.

O Jesus! why can't I tell all *little souls* how unspeakable is Your condescension? I feel that if You found a soul weaker and littler than mine, which is impossible, You would be pleased to grant it still greater favors, provided it abandoned itself with total confidence to Your Infinite Mercy. But why do I desire to communicate Your secrets of Love, O Jesus, for was it not You alone who taught them to me, and can You not reveal them to others? Yes, I know it, and I beg You to do it. I beg You to cast Your Divine Glance upon a great number of *little* souls. I beg You to choose a legion of *little* Victims worthy of Your LOVE!

> *The very little Sister Thérèse of the Child Jesus
> and the Holy Face, unworthy religious of Carmel.*
> — SS 197–200

VALUE OF WEAKNESS

When Thérèse's sister Marie read the letter that contained the above text about the little bird, she wrote back expressing sadness because she was sure that she could never love Jesus as much as Thérèse did. This is Thérèse's consoling reply.

September 17, 1896

Dear Sister, I am not embarrassed in answering you....How can you ask me if it is possible for you to love God as I love Him?...

If you had understood the story of my little bird, you would not have asked me this question. My desires of martyrdom *are nothing;* they are not what give me the unlimited confidence that I feel in my heart. They are, to tell the truth, the spiritual riches that *render one unjust,* when one rests in them with complacence and when one believes they are *something great....* These desires are a *consolation* that Jesus grants at times to weak souls like mine (and these souls are numerous), but when He does not give this *consolation,* it is a grace of *privilege.* Recall those words of Father: "The martyrs suffered with joy, and the King of Martyrs suffered with sadness." Yes, Jesus said: "Father, let this chalice pass away from me." Dear Sister, how can you say after this that my desires are the sign of my love?...Ah! I really feel that it is not this at all that pleases God in my little soul; what pleases Him is *that He sees me loving my littleness* and my *poverty, the blind hope that I have in His mercy....* That is my only treasure, dear Godmother, why would this treasure not be yours?...Are you not ready to suffer all that God will desire? I really know that you are ready; therefore, if you want to feel joy, to have an attraction for suffering, it is your consolation that you are seeking, since when we love a thing the pain disappears. I assure you, if we were to go to martyrdom together in the dispositions we are in now, you would have great merit, and I would have none at all, unless Jesus was pleased to change my dispositions.

Oh, dear Sister, I beg you, understand your little girl, understand that to love Jesus, to be His *victim of love,* the weaker one is, without desires or virtues, the more suited one is for the workings of this consuming and transforming Love.... The *desire* alone to be a victim suffices, but we must consent to remain always poor and without strength, and this is the difficulty, for: "The truly poor in spirit, where do we find him? You must look for him from afar," said the psalmist.... He does not say that you must look for him among great souls, but "from afar," that is to say in *lowliness,* in *nothingness....* Ah! let us remain then *very far* from all that sparkles, let us love our littleness, let us love to feel nothing, then we shall be poor in spirit, and Jesus will come to look for us, and *however far* we may be, He will transform us in flames of love.... Oh, how I would like to be able to make you understand what I feel!... It is confidence and nothing but confidence that must lead us to Love.... Does not fear lead to Justice [To strict justice such as it is portrayed for sinners, but not this Justice that Jesus will have toward those who love Him]?... Since we see the *way*, let us run together. Yes, I feel it, Jesus wills to give us the same graces, He wills to give us His heaven *gratuitously*.

Oh, dear little Sister, if you do not understand me, it is because you are too great a soul....   —LT #197

REMAINING LITTLE BEFORE GOD

About six weeks before Thérèse died, Mother Agnes recorded these words as her response to a request to explain what she meant by "remaining a little child before God."

It is to recognize our nothingness, to expect everything from God as a little child expects everything from its father; it is to be disquieted about nothing, and not to be set on gaining our living. Even among the poor, they give the child what is necessary, but as soon as he grows up, his father no longer wants to feed him and says: "Work now, you can take care of yourself."

It was so as not to hear this that I never wanted to grow up, feeling that I was incapable of making my living, the eternal life of heaven. I've always remained little, therefore, having no other occupation but to gather flowers, the flowers of love and sacrifice, and of offering them to God in order to please Him.

To be little is not attributing to oneself the virtues that one practices, believing oneself capable of anything, but to recognize that God places this treasure in the hands of His little child to be used when necessary; but it remains always God's treasure. Finally, it is not to become discouraged over one's little faults, for children fall often, but they are too little to hurt themselves very much.   August 6, 1897 — LC #135

SLEEP ON THE HEART OF JESUS

This is one of Thérèse's more literal expressions of what it means to practice spiritual childhood.

December 1896

To Sister Marie of Saint Joseph

How naughty to spend one's night in fretting, instead of falling asleep on the Heart of Jesus!...

If the night frightens the little child, if she complains at *not seeing* Him who is carrying her, let her *close her eyes,* let her WILLINGLY make the sacrifice that is asked of her, and then let her await sleep... when she keeps herself peaceful in this way, the night which she is no longer looking at will be unable to frighten her, and soon calm, if not joy, will be reborn in her little heart....

Is it too much to ask the little child to close her eyes?... not to struggle against the chimeras of the night?... No, it is not too much, and the little child *will abandon* herself, she will believe that Jesus is carrying her, she will consent not to see Him and to leave far behind the empty fear of being unfaithful (a fear not fitting for a little child).

An Ambassador
— LT #205

LITTLENESS

Thérèse wrote this note to commemorate the anniversary of her sister Céline's first communion. (Actually, it had been seventeen years earlier; the thirteen years was the time since Thérèse's own first communion.)

May 13, 1897

To Sister Genevieve

Jesus is pleased with little Céline to whom He gave Himself for the first time thirteen years ago. He is more proud of what He is doing in her soul, of her littleness and her poverty, then

He is proud of having created millions of suns and the expanse
of the heavens!... —LT #227

LONGING TO PREACH
MARY'S TRUE SIMPLICITY

*On August 21, just five weeks before Thérèse's death, Mother
Agnes recorded her voicing her distaste for sermons that overly
exalt the Blessed Virgin instead of emphasizing her loving humility and tenderness. Deeply convinced of her own mission to
teach the "little way," Thérèse expresses regret that she could
not have done so as an ordained minister.*

How I would have loved to be a priest in order to preach
about the Blessed Virgin! One sermon would be sufficient to
say everything I think about this subject.

I'd first make people understand how little is known by us
about her life.

We shouldn't say unlikely things or things we don't know
anything about! For example, that when she was very little, at
the age of three, the Blessed Virgin went up to the Temple to
offer herself to God, burning with sentiments of love and extraordinary fervor. While perhaps she went there very simply
out of obedience to her parents.

Again, why say, with reference to the aged Simeon's prophetic words, that the Blessed Virgin had the Passion of Jesus
constantly before her mind from that moment onward? "And
a sword will pierce through your soul also," the old man said
(Luke 2:35). It wasn't for the present, you see, little Mother; it
was a general prediction for the future.

For a sermon on the Blessed Virgin to please me and do me
any good, I must see her real life, not her imagined life. I'm sure
that her real life was very simple. They show her to us as un-
approachable, but they should present her as imitable, bringing
out her virtues, saying that she lived by faith just like ourselves,

giving proofs of this from the Gospel, where we read: "And they did not understand the words which He spoke to them" (Luke 2:50). And that other no less mysterious statement: "His father and mother marveled at what was said about him" (Luke 2:33). This admiration presupposes a certain surprise, don't you think so, little Mother?

We know very well that the Blessed Virgin is Queen of heaven and earth, but she is more Mother than Queen; and we should not say, on account of her prerogatives, that she surpasses all the saints in glory just as the sun at its rising makes the stars disappear from sight. My God! How strange that would be! A mother who makes her children's glory vanish! I myself think just the contrary. I believe she'll increase the splendor of the elect very much.

It's good to speak about her prerogatives, but we should not stop at this, and if, in a sermon, we are obliged from beginning to end to exclaim and say: Ah! Ah!, we would grow tired! Who knows whether some soul would not reach the point of feeling a certain estrangement from a creature so superior and would not say: If things are such, it's better to go and shine as well as one is able in some little corner!

What the Blessed Virgin has more than we have is the privilege of not being able to sin, she was exempt from the strain of original sin; but on the other hand, she wasn't as fortunate as we are, since she didn't have a Blessed Virgin to love. And this is one more sweetness for us and one less sweetness for her!

August 21, 1897 — LC #3

THÉRÈSE'S PRAYER TO MARY

Three weeks before Thérèse died, she wrote this prayer for the Birthday of Mary (September 8).

O Mary, if I were the Queen of Heaven and you were Thérèse, I would want to be Thérèse so that you could be the Queen of Heaven!   — Prayer #21 in RP

THE PRAYER OF A CHILD

Thérèse affirms the tremendous importance of prayer even as she acknowledges her own struggles in this regard. It is in prayer that the "little way" comes to fruition. This passage describes several simple approaches to prayer that anyone can practice.

How great is the power of *Prayer!* One could call it a Queen who has at each instant free access to the King and who is able to obtain whatever she asks. To be heard it is not necessary to read from a book some beautiful formula composed for the occasion. If this were the case, alas, I would have to be pitied! Outside the *Divine Office* which I am very unworthy to recite, I do not have the courage to force myself to search out *beautiful* prayers in books. There are so many of them it really gives me a headache! And each prayer is more *beautiful* than the others. I cannot recite them all and not knowing which to choose, I do like children who do not know how to read, I say very simply to God what I wish to say, without composing beautiful sentences, and He always understands me. For me, prayer is an aspiration of the heart, it is a simple glance directed to heaven, it is a cry of gratitude and love in the midst of trial as well as joy; finally, it is something great, supernatural, which expands my soul and unites me to Jesus.

However, I would not want you to believe, dear Mother, that I recite without devotion the prayers said in common in the choir or the hermitages. On the contrary, I love very much these prayers in common, for Jesus has promised *to be in the midst of those who gather together in His name.* I feel then that the fervor of my Sisters makes up for my lack of fervor; but when alone (I am ashamed to admit it) the recitation of the rosary is more difficult for me than the wearing of an instrument of penance. I feel I have said this so poorly! I force myself in vain to meditate on the mysteries of the rosary; I don't succeed in fixing my mind on them. For a long time I was desolate about this lack of devotion which astonished me, for I love the Blessed Virgin so much that it should be easy for me to recite in her honor prayers which are so pleasing to her. Now I am less desolate; I think that the Queen of heaven, since she is *my MOTHER,* must see my good will and she is satisfied with it.

Sometimes when my mind is in such a great aridity that it is impossible to draw forth one single thought to unite me with God, I very slowly recite an "Our Father" and then the angelic salutation; then these prayers give me great delight; they nourish my soul much more than if I had recited them precipitately a hundred times.   — SS 242–43

GOD'S GENTLENESS

On a day when she was feeling very ill and feverish, Thérèse had reacted with impatience when a sister persisted in asking her help with something after she had already pled her indisposition. In this letter to Mother Agnes, Thérèse reflects on her imperfection and on the gentleness that Jesus manifests toward his wayward children.

May 28, 1897

Dear little Mother, your little girl has again shed sweet tears just now, tears of repentance but more so of gratitude and love. . . . Ah! this evening I showed my *virtue,* my TREASURES of *patience!* . . . And I who preach so well to others!!!!!!!!!!!!!!! I am happy you saw my imperfection. Ah, the good it does me for having been bad! . . . You did not scold your little girl, nevertheless, she deserved it; but your little girl is accustomed to this, your gentleness speaks more to her than severe words; you are the image of God's *mercy* for her. Yes, but . . . Sister St. John the Baptist, on the contrary, is *usually* the image of God's *severity.* Well, I just met her, and instead of passing coldly by my side, she embraced me, saying: (absolutely as though I had been the best girl in the world) "Poor little Sister, I felt sorry for you, I do not want to tire you out, I was wrong, etc., etc. . . . " I, who felt contrition in my heart, was astonished at her not reproaching me in any way.

I know that basically she must find me imperfect; it is because she believes I am going to die that she has spoken this way to me, but it does not matter. I heard only gentle and tender words coming from her mouth, and I found her very good and myself very bad.... When reentering our cell, I was wondering what Jesus was thinking of me, and immediately I recalled these words He addressed one day to the adulterous woman: "Has no one condemned you?" And I, tears in my eyes, answered Him: "No one, Lord.... Neither my little Mother, image of Your tenderness, nor Sister St. John the Baptist, image of Your justice, and I really feel I can go in peace, for You will not condemn me either!..."

Little Mother, why, then, is Good Jesus so *gentle* towards me? Why does He never scold me?... Ah! truly, it is enough to make me die of gratitude and love!...

I am happier for having been imperfect than if, sustained by grace, I had been a model of meekness.... This does me much good to see Jesus is always so gentle, so tender to me!... Ah! from this moment, I know it: yes, all my hopes will be realized... yes, the Lord will do for us marvels that will infinitely surpass our *immense desires!*...

Your *very little* girl,
Thérèse of the Child Jesus
of the Holy Face
—LT #230

"LET US RUN TO THE LAST PLACE"

Thérèse wrote this note after Sister Genevieve (Céline) came to apologize for having been impatient with her during a lengthy picture-taking session.

June 7, 1897

Beloved little Sister, let us never seek what appears great in the eyes of creatures. Solomon, the wisest king who ever was on earth, having considered the different works that occupy men under the sun, painting, sculpture, all the arts, understood that *all* these *things* were *subject* to *envy;* he cried out that they were only vanity and affliction of spirit! ...

The only thing that is not *envied* is the last place; there is, then, only this *last place* which is not vanity and affliction of spirit....

However, "the way of man is not within his power," and we surprise ourselves at times by desiring what sparkles. So let us line up humbly among the imperfect, let us esteem ourselves as *little souls* whom God must sustain at each moment. When He sees we are very much convinced of our nothingness, He extends His hand to us. If we still wish to attempt doing something *great* even under the pretext of zeal, Good Jesus leaves us all alone. "But when I said: 'My foot has stumbled,' your mercy, Lord, strengthened me!...Ps. 93." Yes, it suffices to humble oneself, to bear with one's imperfections. That is real sanctity! Let us take each other by the hand, dear little sister, and let us run to the last place...no one will come to dispute with us over it....   —LT #243

7

Thérèse,
Spiritual Sister and Missionary

From an early age, Thérèse dreamed of being a missionary. She also made no secret of her frustrated sense of vocation to the priesthood. Even as her illness increasingly sapped her strength, she still hoped for a miraculous cure so that she could go on the Lisieux Carmel's mission in Hanoi. Instead, however, she found that during this life one of the most important ways that the concreteness of her missionary and priestly vocation was to be fulfilled was by her relationship with two "spiritual brothers."

The first, the seminarian Maurice Bellière, was given to her by her prioress in October 1895. About six months later she was asked to take a second spiritual brother, Père Adolphe Roulland. At the same time, she was deeply engaged in her work as auxiliary novice director. She experienced a profound sense of responsibility for the formation and care of all those entrusted to her.

It is in her letters to her spiritual brothers, many of them written during a period when her physical agony was at its peak, that Thérèse most fully articulated her growing insight into the unique character of her own mission — a mission that was by no means to end with her death. In fact, in 1927 Thérèse's missionary vocation came to new fullness when the Holy See gave her the title of "patroness of all missions."

157

Yet the apostolic fruitfulness that has flowed forth from Thérèse's entry into the Communion of Saints overflows even those bounds. She wrote of drawing many along in her train and of continuing her work from heaven; and millions of people throughout the world today offer testimony that she has done just that.

"DRAW ME"

In these, the very last pages of Story of a Soul, *Thérèse shares the core wisdom she has learned about the formation of souls and the fulfillment of mission.*

Since I have two brothers and my little Sisters, the novices, if I wanted to ask for each soul what each one needed and go into detail about it, the days would not be long enough and I fear I would forget something important. For simple souls there must be no complicated ways; as I am of their number, one morning during my thanksgiving, Jesus gave me a simple means of accomplishing my mission.

He made me understand these words of the Canticle of Canticles: *"DRAW ME, WE SHALL RUN after you in the odor of your ointments."* O Jesus, it is not even necessary to say: *"When drawing me, draw the souls whom I love!"* This simple statement: "Draw me" suffices; I understand, Lord, that when a soul allows herself to be captivated by *the odor of your ointments,* she cannot run alone, all the souls whom she loves follow in her train; this is done without constraint, without effort, it is a natural consequence of her attraction for You. Just as a torrent, throwing itself with impetuosity into the ocean, drags after it everything it encounters in its passage, in the same way, O Jesus, the soul who plunges into the shoreless ocean of Your Love, draws with her all the treasures she possesses. Lord, You know it, I have no other treasures than the souls it has pleased You to unite to mine; it is You who entrusted these treasures to me, and so I dare to borrow the words You addressed to the heavenly Father, the last night which saw You on our earth as a traveler and a mortal. Jesus, I do not know when my exile will be ended; more than one night will still see me singing Your Mercies in this exile, but for me will finally come the last night, and then I want to be able to say to You, O my God:

"I have glorified you on earth; I have finished the work you gave me to do. And now do you, Father, glorify me with yourself, with the glory I had with you before the world existed." ...

Mother, I think it is necessary to give a few more explanations on the passage in the Canticle of Canticles: *"Draw me, we shall run,"* for what I wanted to say appears to me little understood. *"No man can come after me, unless the FATHER who sent me draw him,"* Jesus has said. Again, through beautiful parables, and often even without using this means so well known to the people, He teaches us that it is enough to knock and it will be opened, to seek in order to find, and to hold out one's hand humbly to receive what is asked for. He also says that everything we ask the *Father in His name*, He will grant it. No doubt, it is because of this teaching that the Holy Spirit, before Jesus' birth, dictated this prophetic prayer: *"Draw me, we shall run."*

What is it then to ask to be *"Drawn"* if not to be united in an intimate way to the object which captivates our heart? If fire and iron had the use of reason, and if the latter said to the other: "Draw me," would it not prove that it desires to be identified with the fire in such a way that the fire penetrate and drink it up with its burning substance and seem to become one with it? Dear Mother, this is my prayer. I ask Jesus to draw me into the flames of His love, to unite me so closely to Him that He live and act in me. I feel that the more the fire of love burns within my heart, the more I shall say: *"Draw me,"* the more also the souls who will approach me (poor little piece of iron, useless if I withdraw from the divine furnace), the more these souls *will run swiftly in the odor of the ointments of their*

Beloved, for a soul that is burning with love cannot remain inactive. No doubt, she will remain at Jesus' feet as did Mary
Magdalene, and she will listen to His sweet and burning words.
Appearing to do nothing, she will give much more than Martha
who torments herself with many things and wants her sister to
imitate her. It is not Martha's works that Jesus finds fault with;
His divine Mother submitted humbly to these works all through
her life since she had to prepare the meals of the Holy Family.
It is only the restlessness of His ardent hostess that He willed
to correct.

All the saints have understood this, and more especially those
who filled the world with the light of the Gospel teachings.
Was it not in prayer that St. Paul, St. Augustine, St. John of
the Cross, St. Thomas Aquinas, St. Francis, St. Dominic, and so
many other famous Friends of God have drawn out this divine
science which delights the greatest geniuses? A scholar has said:
"Give me a lever and a fulcrum and I will lift the world." What
Archimedes was not able to obtain, for his request was not directed by God and was only made from a material viewpoint,
the saints have obtained in all its fullness. The Almighty has
given them as *fulcrum: HIMSELF ALONE; as lever:* PRAYER
which burns with a fire of love. And it is in this way that they
have *lifted the world;* it is in this way that the saints still militant lift it, and that, until the end of time, the saints to come
will lift it.

Dear Mother, now I would like to tell you what I understand
by the *odor of the ointments* of the Beloved. Since Jesus has re-
ascended into heaven, I can follow Him only in the traces He
has left; but how luminous these traces are! how perfumed! I
have only to cast a glance in the Gospels and immediately I
breathe in the perfumes of Jesus' life, and I know on which side
to run. I don't hasten to the first place but to the last; rather
than advance like the Pharisee, I repeat, filled with confidence,
the publican's humble prayer. Most of all I imitate the conduct
of Magdalene; her astonishing or rather her loving audacity
which charms the Heart of Jesus also attracts my own. Yes, I

feel it; even though I had on my conscience all the sins that can be committed, I would go, my heart broken with sorrow, and throw myself into Jesus' arms, for I know how much He loves the prodigal child who returns to Him. It is not because God, in His anticipating Mercy, has preserved my soul from mortal sin that I go to Him with confidence and love.. . .

— SS 254–55, 257–59

THE CHARACTER OF
THE APOSTOLIC VOCATION

In this letter of November 1, 1896, Thérèse tells Père Roulland of her amazement at discovering that a prayer she offered on her profession day six years earlier had, unbeknownst to her, been answered that very day. She celebrates the Providence of God, which has prepared their relationship long before the day of their encounter. In this letter she also describes with great clarity her vision of the apostolic vocation.

I cannot tell you, Brother, how happy I am to see you so totally abandoned into your superiors' hands. It seems to me it is a certain proof that one day my desires will be realized, that is, that you will be a great Saint. Allow me to confide a secret to you that was just revealed to me by the sheet of paper on which are written the memorable dates of your life. On September 8, 1890, your missionary vocation was saved by Mary, Queen of Apostles and Martyrs; on that same day, a little Carmelite became the spouse of the King of heaven. Bidding an everlasting *adieu* to the world, she had one goal, to save souls, especially the souls of apostles. From Jesus, her divine Spouse, she asked particularly for an apostolic soul; unable to be a priest, she wanted that in her place a priest may receive the graces of the Lord, that he have the same aspirations, the same desires as herself.. . .

Brother, you know the unworthy Carmelite who offered this prayer. Do you not think, as I do, that our union confirmed on the day of your priestly ordination began on September 8?...I believed I would meet only in heaven the apostle, the brother whom I had asked from Jesus; but this Beloved Savior, raising a little the mysterious veil that hides the secrets of eternity, has seen fit to give me in this exile the consolation of knowing the brother of my soul, of working with him for the salvation of poor infidels.

Oh! how great is my gratitude when I consider the kind attention of Jesus!...What is He reserving for us in heaven if here below His love dispenses surprises so delightful?

More than ever, I understand that the smallest events of our life are conducted by God; He is the One who makes us desire and who grants our desires....When our good Mother suggested to me that I become your helper, I admit, Brother, that I hesitated. Considering the virtues of the holy Carmelites around us, I thought that our Mother would have better served your spiritual interests by choosing for you a Sister other than myself; the thought alone that Jesus would have no regard for my imperfect works but for my good will made me accept the honor of sharing in your apostolic works. I did not know then that Our Lord Himself had chosen me, He who uses the weakest instruments to work marvels!...I did not know that for six years I had a *brother* who was preparing himself to become a missionary; now that this brother is really His apostle, Jesus reveals it to me in order no doubt to increase in my soul the desire of loving Him and making Him loved.

Do you know, Brother, that if the Lord *continues* to answer my prayer, you will obtain a favor which your humility prevents you from seeking? This incomparable favor, you guess it, is martyrdom....

Yes, I have the hope that after *long* years spent in apostolic works, after having given Jesus love for love, life for life, you will give Him, too, blood for blood....

When writing these lines, I am reminded that they will reach you in the month of January, the month during which we exchange happy wishes. I believe that those of your little sister will be the only ones of their kind. . . . To tell the truth, the world would treat as folly wishes like these; however, for us the world no longer lives, and "our conversation is already in heaven," our only desire is to resemble our adorable Master, whom the world did not wish to know because He emptied Himself, taking on the form and nature of a slave. On, Brother! how blessed you are to follow so closely the example of Jesus! . . .

—LT #201

A UNION OF SOULS

This letter, written to Abbé Bellière on Ash Wednesday of 1897, is one of the first in which Thérèse speaks of how her mission will continue after her death.

Before entering into the silence of holy Lent, I want to add a short note to our Reverend Mother's letter to thank you for the one you sent me last month.

If you experience any consolation when you think that in Carmel a Sister is praying incessantly for you, my gratitude is not less great than yours to Our Lord, who has given me a little brother whom He destines to become His priest and His apostle. . . . Truly, you will know only in heaven how dear you are to me; I feel our souls are made to understand one another. Your prose which you call "rough and ready" reveals to me that Jesus has placed in you aspirations that He gives only to souls called to the highest sanctity. Since He Himself has chosen me to be your sister, I trust He will not look upon my weakness or rather that He will use this weakness even to carry out His work, for the strong God loves to show His power by making use of nothing. United in Him, our souls will be able to save many others, for this gentle Jesus has said: "If two among you agree together on something which you ask from my Father, it will be granted them." Ah! what we are asking Him is to work for His glory, to love Him and make Him loved.... How would our union and our prayer not be blessed? ...

You tell me that very often you pray also for your sister; since you have this charity, I would be very happy if each day you would consent to offer this prayer for her which contains all her desires: "Merciful Father, in the name of our gentle Jesus, the Virgin Mary, and the Saints, I beg you to enkindle my sister with Your Spirit of Love and to grant her the favor of making You loved very much." You have promised to pray for me *throughout your life;* no doubt your life will be longer than mine, and it is not permitted you to sing like me: "I have the hope my exile will be short! ... " but neither are you permitted to forget your promise. If the Lord takes me soon with Him, I ask you to continue each day the same prayer, for I shall desire in heaven the same thing as I do on earth: To love Jesus and to make Him loved.

Monsieur l'Abbé, you must think I am very strange; perhaps you are sorry to have a sister who seems to want to go and enjoy repose and leave you working alone.... But rest assured, the only thing I desire is God's will, and I admit that if in heaven I were no longer to work for His glory, I would prefer exile to the homeland.

I do not know the future; however, if Jesus realizes my presentiments, I promise to remain your little sister up above. Our union, far from being broken, will become more intimate. Then there will no longer be any cloister and grilles, and my soul will be able to fly with you into distant missions. Our roles will remain the same: yours, apostolic weapons, mine, prayer and love.   —LT #220

WAITING FOR TRANSFORMATION

On April 25, 1897, Thérèse wrote to Abbé Bellière about her awareness of her absolute need for God's transforming mercy.

...Dear little Brother, I must admit that in your letter there is something that caused me some sorrow, and it is that you do not know me such as I am in reality. It is true that to find great souls one must come to Carmel; just as in virgin forests there grow flowers of a fragrance and brilliance unknown to the world, so Jesus in His mercy has willed that among these flowers there should grow littler ones; never will I be able to thank Him enough, for it is thanks to this condescension that I, a poor flower without splendor, find myself in the same garden as the roses, my Sisters. Oh, Brother! I beg you to believe me. God has not given you as a sister a *great* soul but a *very little* and a very imperfect one.

Do not think that it is humility that prevents me from acknowledging the gifts of God. I know He has done great things in me, and I sing of this each day with joy. I remember that the one must love more who has been forgiven more, so I take care to make my life an act of love, and I am no longer disturbed at being a *little* soul; on the contrary, I take delight in this. That is why I dare to hope "my exile will be short," but it is not because I am *prepared.* I feel that I shall never be prepared if the Lord does not see fit to transform me Himself. He can do so in one instant; after all the graces He has granted me, I still await this one from His infinite mercy.   —LT #224

THE WAY OF CONFIDENCE AND LOVE

Writing to Père Roulland on May 9, Thérèse vehemently disagreed with the harsh views of God's justice that were being taught by many of her contemporaries. She also mentions Théophane Vénard, a young priest-martyr to whom she had great devotion during the final months of her life.

...On this earth, where all changes, one single thing remains, and this is the conduct of the King of heaven regarding His friends. Ever since He has lifted up the standard of the Cross, it is under its shadow that all must fight and carry off the victory. Théophane Vénard said: "The whole of a missionary's life is fruitful in the Cross;" and again, "To be truly happy we must suffer, and to love we must die." . . .

I do not understand, Brother, how you seem to doubt your immediate entrance into heaven if the infidels were to take your life. I know one must be very pure to appear before the God of all Holiness, but I know, too, that the Lord is infinitely just; and it is this justice which frightens so many souls that is the object of my joy and confidence. To be just is not only to exercise severity in order to punish the guilty; it is also to recognize right intentions and to reward virtue. I expect as much from God's justice as from His mercy. It is because He is just that "He is compassionate and filled with gentleness, slow to punish, and abundant in mercy, for He knows our frailty, He remembers we are only dust. As a father has tenderness for his children, so the Lord has compassion on us!!" Oh, Brother, when hearing these beautiful and consoling words of the Prophet-King, how can we doubt that God will open the doors of His kingdom to His children who loved Him even to sacrificing all for Him, who have not only left their family and their country to make Him known and loved, but even desire to give their life for Him whom they love. . . . Jesus was very right in saying that there is no greater love than that! How would He allow Himself to be overcome in generosity? How would He purify in the flames of purgatory souls consumed in the fires of divine love? It is true that no human life is exempt from faults; only the Immaculate Virgin presents herself absolutely pure before the divine Majesty. What a joy to think that this Virgin is our Mother! Since she loves us and since she knows our weakness, what have we to fear? Here are a lot of sentences to express my thought, or rather not to succeed in expressing it, I wanted simply to say that it seems to me all missionaries are *martyrs* by desire and will and that, as a consequence, not one should have to go to purgatory. If there remains in their soul at the moment of appearing before God some trace of human weakness, the Blessed Virgin obtains for them the grace of making an act of perfect love, and then she gives them the palm and the crown that they so greatly merited.

This is, Brother, what I think of God's justice; my way is all confidence and love. I do not understand souls who fear a Friend so tender. At times, when I am reading certain spiritual treatises in which perfection is shown through a thousand obstacles, surrounded by a crowd of illusions, my poor little mind quickly tires; I close the learned book that is breaking my head and drying up my heart, and I take up Holy Scripture. Then all seems luminous to me; a single word uncovers for my soul infinite horizons, perfection seems simple to me, I see it is sufficient to recognize one's nothingness and to abandon oneself as a child into God's arms. Leaving to great souls, to great minds the beautiful books I cannot understand, much less put into practice, I rejoice at being little since children alone and those who resemble them will be admitted to the heavenly banquet. I am very happy there are many mansions in God's kingdom, for if there were only the one whose description and road seems incomprehensible to me, I would not be able to enter there. I would like, however, not to be too far from *your mansion;* in consideration of your merits, I hope God will give me the favor of sharing in your glory, just as on earth the sister of a conqueror, were she deprived of the gifts of nature, shares in the honors bestowed on her brother in spite of her own poverty.

—LT #226

THE "LITTLE ZERO"

The end of the same letter offers another image of how Thérèse understood the apostolic power of her "little way."

...If, as I believe, my father and mother are in heaven, they must be looking at and blessing the brother whom Jesus has given me. They had so much wanted a missionary son!...I have been told that before my birth my parents were hoping their prayer was finally going to be realized. Had they been able to pierce through the veil of the future, they would have seen it was indeed through me their desire was fulfilled; since a missionary has become my brother, he is also their son, and in their prayers they cannot separate the brother from his unworthy sister.

. . . How sweet will be the family life we shall enjoy throughout eternity! While awaiting this blessed eternity that will open up for us in a short time, since life is only a day, let us work together for the salvation of souls. I can do very little, or rather absolutely nothing, if I am alone; what consoles me is to think that at your side I can be useful for something. In fact, zero by itself has no value, but when placed next to a unit it becomes powerful, provided, however, that it be placed on the *right side,* after and not before! . . . That is where Jesus has placed me, and I hope to remain there always, following you from a distance by prayer and sacrifice.

If I were to listen to my heart, I would not end my letter today, but the end of silence is about to ring. I must bring my letter to our good Mother, who is waiting for it. I beg you, then, Brother, to send your blessing to the *little zero* God has placed near you.   —LT #226

"I REALLY COUNT ON NOT REMAINING INACTIVE IN HEAVEN"

When Thérèse wrote her last letter to Père Roulland on July 14, she believed that her death was imminent. For her the veil between earth and heaven was already rent; she was increasingly possessed by the conviction of continuity between her mission now and after death.

You tell me in your last letter (which pleased me very much): "I am a *baby* who is learning to talk." Well, I, for the last five or six weeks, am a baby too, for I am living only on *milk;* but soon I shall sit down at the heavenly banquet, I shall quench my thirst at the waters of eternal life! When you receive this letter, no doubt I shall have left this earth. The Lord in His infinite mercy will have opened His kingdom to me, and I shall be able to draw from His treasures in order to grant them liberally to the souls who are dear to me. Believe, Brother, that your little sister will hold to her promises, and, her soul, freed from the weight of the mortal envelope, will joyfully fly toward the distant regions that you are evangelizing. Ah! Brother, I feel it, I shall be more useful to you in heaven than on earth, and it is with joy that I come to announce to you my coming entrance into that blessed city, sure that you will share my joy and will thank the Lord for giving me the means of helping you more effectively in your apostolic works. I really count on not remaining inactive in heaven. My desire is to work still for the Church and for souls. I am asking God for this and I am certain He will answer me. Are not the angels continually occupied with us without their ever ceasing to see the divine Face and to lose themselves in the Ocean of Love without shores? Why would Jesus not allow me to imitate them?

Brother, you see that if I am leaving the field of battle already, it is not with the selfish desire of taking my rest. The thought of eternal beatitude hardly thrills my heart. For a long time, suffering has become my heaven here below, and I really have trouble in conceiving how I shall be able to acclimatize myself in a country where joy reigns without any admixture of sadness. Jesus will have to transform my soul and give it the capacity to rejoice, otherwise I shall not be able to put up with eternal delights.

What attracts me to the homeland of heaven is the Lord's call, the hope of loving Him finally as I have so much desired to love Him, and the thought that I shall be able to make Him loved by a multitude of souls who will bless Him eternally.

—LT #254

THE HALF-EXTINGUISHED LAMP

Mother Agnes recorded this story in the "Last Conversations" of July 15, 1897. By this time Thérèse was so ill that the doctors believed she might die at any time; she was, quite literally, "a half-extinguished lamp." The story poignantly expresses Thérèse's understanding of the character and fruitfulness of her ongoing mission as "love in the heart of the Church."

Sister Marie of the Eucharist wanted to light the candles for a procession; she had no matches; however, seeing the little lamp which was burning in the front of the relics, she approached it. Alas, it was half out; there remained only a feeble glimmer on its blackened wick. She succeeded in lighting her candle from it, and with this candle, she lighted those of the whole community. It was, therefore, the half-extinguished little lamp which had produced all these beautiful flames which, in their turn, could produce an infinity of others and even light the whole universe. Nevertheless, it would always be the little lamp which would be first cause of all this light. How could the beautiful flames boast of having produced this fire, when they themselves were lighted with such a small spark?

It is the same with the Communion of Saints. Very often, without our knowing it, the graces and lights that we receive are due to a hidden soul, for God wills that the saints communicate grace to each other through prayer with great love, with a love much greater than that of a family, and even the most perfect family on earth. How often have I thought that I may owe all the graces I've received to the prayers of a person who begged them from God for me, and whom I shall know only in heaven.

Yes, a very little spark will be capable of giving birth to great lights in the Church, like the Doctors and Martyrs, who will undoubtedly be higher in heaven than the spark; but how could anyone think that their glory will not become his?

In heaven, we shall not meet with indifferent glances, because all the elect will discover that they owe to each other the graces that merited the crown for them.   —LC pp. 99–100

THE BALM OF CONSOLATION

Abbé Bellière often suffered from melancholy and doubt, and Thérèse's announcement of her impending death only added to his misery. In her reply on July 18, Thérèse made a supreme effort to comfort and instruct him.

...I undoubtedly explained myself poorly in my last note, since you tell me, very dear little Brother, "not to ask from you this *joy* I feel at the approach of *bliss*." Ah, if for a few moments you could read into my soul, how surprised you would be. The thought of heavenly bliss not only causes me not a single bit of joy, but I even ask myself at times how it will be possible to be happy without any suffering. Jesus no doubt will change my nature, otherwise I would miss suffering and the valley of tears. Never have I asked God to die young, this would have appeared to me as cowardliness; but He, from my childhood, saw fit to give me the intimate conviction that my course here below would be short. It is, then, the thought alone of accomplishing the Lord's will that makes up all my joy.

Oh, little Brother, how I would like to be able to pour into your heart the balm of consolation! I can only borrow the words of Jesus at the Last Supper. He cannot take offense at this since I am His little spouse and, consequently, His goods are mine. I say to you, then, as He said to His intimate friends: "I am going to my Father, but because I have spoken to you these things, sorrow has filled your heart. But I speak the truth to you: it is expedient for you that I depart. And you, therefore, have sorrow now; but I will see you again, and your heart will rejoice, and your joy no one will take from you."

Yes, I am certain of it, after my entrance into life, *my dear little Brother's* sadness will be changed into a *peaceful joy* that no creature will be able to take from him. I feel it, we must go to heaven by the same way, that of suffering united to love. When I shall be in port, I shall teach you, dear little Brother of my soul, how you must sail the stormy sea of the world with the abandonment and the love of a child who knows his Father loves him and would be unable to leave him in the hour of danger. Ah! how I would like to make you understand the tenderness of the Heart of Jesus, what He expects from you. In your letter of the fourteenth, you made my heart thrill sweetly; I understood more than ever the degree to which your soul is sister to my own, since it is called to raise itself to God by the ELEVATOR of love and not to climb the rough *stairway* of fear....I am not surprised in any way that the practice of familiarity with Jesus seems to you a little difficult to realize; we cannot reach it in one day, but I am sure that I shall help you much more to walk by this delightful way when I shall have been delivered from my mortal envelope, and soon, like St. Augustine, you will say: "Love is the weight that draws me."

I would like to try to make you understand by means of a very simple comparison how much Jesus loves even imperfect souls who confide in Him:

I picture a father who has two children, mischievous and disobedient, and when he comes to punish them, he sees one of them who trembles and gets away from him in terror, having, however, in the bottom of his heart the feeling that he deserves to be punished; and his brother, on the contrary, throws himself into his father's arms, saying that he is sorry for having caused him any trouble, that he loves him, and to prove it he will be good from now on, and if this child asks his father to punish him with a *kiss,* I do not believe that the heart of the happy father could resist the filial confidence of his child, whose sincerity and love he knows. He realizes, however, that more than once his son will fall into the same faults, but he is prepared to pardon him always, if his son always takes him by his heart....I say nothing to you about the first child, dear little Brother, you must know whether his father can love him as much and treat him with the same indulgence as the other.... —LT #258

"A DIEU, DEAR LITTLE BROTHER"

This is the last letter of any length which Thérèse was able to write. It was sent to Abbé Bellière on August 10, 1897. In fact, she lived another three weeks; she made her final passage on the evening of September 30, after a terrible agony lasting two full days.

I am now all ready to leave; I received my passport for heaven and my dear father is the one who obtained this grace for me. On the 29th he gave me the assurance that I was soon to join him; the next day, the doctor, surprised at the progress the sickness had made in two days, told our good Mother that it was time to grant my desires by having me receive Extreme Unction. I had this happiness, then, on the 30th, and also that of seeing Jesus-Victim leave the tabernacle for me, whom I received as *Viaticum* for my *long* voyage!... This Bread of Heaven fortified me; see, my pilgrimage seems to be unable to end. Far from complaining about it, I rejoice that God permits me to suffer still for His love; ah! how sweet it is to abandon oneself into His arms without fear or desire.

I admit to you, little Brother, that we do not understand heaven in the same way. It seems to you that sharing in the justice, in the holiness of God, I would be unable as on earth to excuse your faults. Are you forgetting, then, that I shall be sharing also in the infinite mercy of the Lord? I believe the Blessed have great compassion on our miseries, they remember, being weak and mortal like us, they committed the same faults, sustained the same combats, and their fraternal tenderness becomes greater than it was when they were on earth, and for this reason, they never cease protecting us and praying for us....

A *Dieu*, dear little Brother; may He give us the grace to love Him and save souls for Him. This is the wish that your unworthy little Sister Thérèse of the Child Jesus of the Holy Face has.

—LT #263